RUNNIN' WITH
FROGs

A NAVY MEMOIR

George R. Worthington

ISBN: 978-1-64314-626-3 (Paperback)
      978-1-64314-071-1 (Hardback)

AuthorsPress
California, USA
www.authorspress.com

CONTENTS

REAR ADMIRAL GEORGE R. WORTHINGTON, U.S. NAVY (RETIRED)

Rear Admiral George R. Worthington, USN (Ret.) was born on July 11, 1937, in Louisville, Kentucky. The family bounced around during the war years from Florida to Texas while his father served in the Navy. In 1948 they settled in Rockaway Park, Long Island, until 1950. Worthington was sent to South Kent School while the family moved to Tucson. He attended a year at Brown University until receiving an appointment to the U.S. Naval Academy where he graduated with the class of 1961.

His first active assignment was in USS HALSEY POWELL (DD-686). Strong participated in the 1962 nuclear bomb tests off Christmas Island in the South Pacific. A follow-on assignment was as Flag Lieutenant and Aide to Commander Cruiser-Destroyer Flotilla SEVEN operating out of San Diego. Early in this position he participated in the International Naval Pentathlon in Sweden, and later as a member of the Military Sport Council swimming competition in Barcelona. He rejoined the Flotilla in Subic Bay in September.

Worthington attended Underwater Demolition Training from July to December 1965, after which he was assigned as Operations Officer of UDT-11. The Team was deployed to Subic Bay in April 1966, where the Team embarked to participate in Operation Jackstay. Following two years and two deployments with UDT-11, Worthington attended Destroyer Department Head School and reported from graduation to U.S.S. Strong (DD-758) homeported in Charleston. A Sixth Fleet deployment with two Black Sea transits was followed by assignment to Vietnam on the NAVFORV Naval Special Warfare Group (Vietnam).

Command of SEAL Team ONE followed in 1972, followed by a tour as Naval Attache to Cambodia, Marine Corps Command and Staff College, command of Inshore Undersea Warfare Group ONE—where he initiated efforts to develop Naval Special Warfare Command and Control Communications vans—National War College, and a six-year stint Pentagon Navy Staff during an exciting period of Special Operations growth. Worthington sponsored a Naval Special Warfare Master Plan that played a part in financing SEAL Teams. He later initiated work to commission a Naval Special Warfare Training Center as a major command.

Order as Commander Navel Special Warfare Group ONE came in 1985. Follow-on assignment was with the Special Operations Command, Europe in Stuttgart, Germany. Flag selection led back to Washington as Deputy Assistant Secretary of Defense for Special Operations, which at that time meant working directly for the Secretary of the Army and liaison with the Joint Staffs and included an opportunity to brief Joint Service Chiefs on Navy SEAL organization and development.

Following duty in Special Operations/Low Intensity Conflict (SOLIC), Worthington took command of the Naval Special Warfare

Command in Coronado. He served three years in retirement in August 1992. Worthington is an all-American master swimmer and former sports parachutist with a "D" license from the United States Parachute Association. He has three children, one of whom serves as a SEAL.

FOREWORD
"RUNNIN' WITH FROGS – A NAVY MEMOIR"

My first exposure to Navy "Frogmen," the illustrious World War II beach marauders, during a 1959 Naval Academy summer excursion to Little Creek, Virginia, to get briefed up on Navy-Marine Corps Amphibious capabilities. The Academy crammed in a one-hour presentation by a First Class Petty Officer, who started off his presentation with an M-80 firecracker in a wastebasket. Bleary-eyed, hungover Midshipmen were immediately hoisted onto the edges of their seats wondering what the next surprise would be. The next fifty minutes, followed by ten Q&A, went spellbindingly fast. No one had any intention of becoming a Frogman after graduation. In fact, officers had to serve two years of shipboard duty before even applying for Underwater Demolition Team Training (UDTRA). And more than one tour in the Teams was frowned on. Academy graduates run ships not rubber boats called "Inflatable Boat, Small (IBS)."

"Command at Sea" was the hallmark of a naval career—except, of course, those Midshipmen selected for the Marine Corps. Still, the sailor's pitch was entertaining; the closest thing we would get to an IBS was with the Marine Recon Company, a couple of hours paddling around the beach. Rare indeed was the Academy Frogman—and I will cite this fact later with a couple of exceptions.

My next encounter with Frogs, was during the summer of 1963. By then I was the Flag Lieutenant and Aide to a Flotilla Commander. He enlisted me for the tryouts for the Naval Pentathlon Team scheduled to go to Sweden the last week of August. "Aye, aye, Sir, I'll give it my best shot"—about which more later too. I did the test swim and run and made the invite list to win selection. I was selected to participate. All the contestants were Team guys, except for one Marine, 1ˢᵗ Lt. Gordie Collette, an Oklahoma National Breaststroke Champion. The training was conducted at the U.S. Naval Amphibious Base, Coronado, California; and managed by Underwater Demolition Team TWELVE. The next two months was close quarters with Frogmen and a Marine. (We were the only officers on the Pentathlon Team.) I did quite a bit of "Running with Frogs" in 1963. The pentathlon consisted of an obstacle course, a seamanship course, two swimming courses, and a cross-country obstacle/shooting event. The Swedes and Norsemen had been practicing it for years; us, two months. There are learned tricks of the trade.

After all the games—which included the September swim competition—I made it back to Command in Subic Bay, The Philippines. On the fight out I met the commanding officer to UDT-12, 1953 USNA grad Lieutenant Bill Robinson. As a LT (j.g.) (Lieutenant Junior Grade) and a 1961 grad, I was deemed fit to associate with even the rank difference. We enjoyed a festive evening at the Clark Officers' Club. With a two-hour bus ride to Subic, I checked into the COMCRUDESFLOT SEVEN Flagship—the "Conquering Hero" returns. Well, I did win the All

Navy Championship and ended up ninth in the world. So, "Running with Frogs" I did.

After the pentathlon I returned to being an Aide. We made on swing-through pass into Vietnamese waters then prepared to steam home. Two days out of Pearl Harbor President Kennedy was shot. He had spoken at my class graduation. We held a soft spot for him.

We pulled into San Diego right before 1963 Thanksgiving. As a bachelor, I got staff duty. We had a new commander, which was not unusual, 1964 was routinely boring with changes of command to attend and various waterfront administrative functions. It was during this time I decided to apply for UDTRA. "'Boo, hiss,' from the back bench of senior staffers." The acapella chorus sang, "bad career move." But I had spent a lot of social time with Team officers. Robinson even peeked in on my chamber pressure test for oxygen tolerance at depth. In short, I knew a lot of the guys. In fact, there was just beginning the start of a Masters' Program headquartered at the Naval Training Center, which sponsored several swim meets. I roped several Frogs into swimming. So, I was a known quantity. I was headed for "Runnin' with Frogs."

There's a lot of "runnin'" in UDT (now SEAL Teams.) But as I use the term "runnin'" means working with, drinking with, hanging out with, serving with, and alongside with; looking after teammates, and acquiring the skills necessary for service in Naval Special Warfare (then UDTs and SEALS). (And don't forget the boats!) The learning curve started in UDTRA, where volunteers learned the techniques of beach and hydrographic reconnaissance, hinterland surveillance, basic demolitions (hydrographic and land), and safety small arms (greatly expanded today's SEAL Teams), rudimentary patrolling, and land navigation, weather, tides (hydrography), celestial impact, parachuting, underwater ship attacks, and—as Vietnam involvement expanded—enemy leadership confrontation. There was a lot to learn that went in a different direction than driving ships—fleet operations. My first two active years were in destroyers (then UDTRA), and two years in UDT-11, then Destroyer Department Head School ("DESTECH"), two more in the Fleet as a destroyer department head responsible for plans, ship exercises, communications and electronics, and the Combat Information Center (CIC). I was Officer of the Deck for General Quarters, Sea and Anchor Detail, and sundry other at-sea events. Not much to do with beach recons or taking out VC. But other than six years in Surface Warfare, all my "runnin'" was with Naval Special Warfare in a Team, on sundry staffs, in command in "04, 05, 06, 07" paygrades, or in professional schools supportive of follow-on assignment: (now) BUD/S, Destroyers, Attache', and two War Colleges—U.S.M.C. Command & Staff and The National War College.

I lament not achieving a master's degree and admire those able to hold down a day job in the Pentagon and pursue night courses. All of my staff slots were Team related. The excitement of "runnin'" with Frogs from a Pentagon perch (1979–1985) lay in the advancing accrual of relevance not just inside the building but in the Geographic Commands. I mention the era as a source of pride of accomplishment as adeptly related by Susan L. Marquis in her 1997 comprehensive study titled *Unconventional WARFARE: Rebuilding U.S. Special Operations Forces* (Brookings Institution Press, Washington D.C.).

Marquis captures the caustic period succinctly and thoroughly, touching on Pentagon and Congressional leadership; the former resistant to change, the latter determined to fix it. From my perspective on the Navy Staff, there was little interest growing SEALS. Then

DESERT ONE in Iran. Army and Air Force took most of the heat and all of the casualties—not to mention the Carter Administration, whose days were numbered. In truth, on the Navy Staff we were making modest gains, e.g., stood up UK-based Naval Special Warfare Unit TWO in Scotland; procured needed oxygen scuba, and a new suite of small arms. In 1982 we published a Naval Special Warfare Master Plan—a full year before the SECDEF initiative of October 3, 1983, revitalizing Special Operations Forces—an effort that appears ongoing. We'll cover this in more detail. My whole point is "Runnin' with Frogs" entailed more than kicking up road dust; it meant runnin' through the halls of Pentagon, the far reaches to Congress—House started, Senate nailed it, and throughout the Service at home and abroad. The Senate legislative brush touched not just the home base, but sprinkled SOF stars of the Combatant Commands. Looking back, the eighties were robust with Special Operations initiatives and several armed clashes. It was an exciting experience to be a part of. As I commence my review, events are noted from my perspective. And, finally, at the end of each chapter I will estimate what I learned from the tour. "Runnin' with Frogs" became my service calling.

Finally, I am breaking this memoir into three phases—where I was, what happened, my reaction, and what I learned:

i. The early years—life and schooling; getting ready.
ii. Active duty in the U.S. Navy—two warfare specialties with assignments in state and defense departments.
iii. The rest of it—living, still learning, paying attention.

CHAPTER 1

THE EARLY YEARS: 1937-1956

The varied opportunities and experiences I had in the U.S. Navy were personally expansive and rewarding, examples of which might be observing two nuclear air blasts off Christmas Island in the South Pacific (1962), sloshing in a mangrove swamp in Vietnam (1966), conning destroyer alongside a supply ship in the middle of the night (1970), jumping out of an Air Force C-130 at 20,000 feet over Taiwan (1967), sitting daily with the Chief of Naval Operations of the Cambodian Navy (1975), briefing the Joint Service Chiefs "in the Tank" in the bowls of the Pentagon (1984), briefing congressmen and senators on Navy SEAL programs (Skelton and McCain, 1975), standing at the elbow of the General heading NATO (1988), and getting occasionally chewed out by the best along the way. You take all, rejoice for good results, and learn from the rest. And it's more than simply keeping your nose clean, as my World War II B-25 bomber pilot uncle challenged me a long time ago. He flew in China with a Chinese crew. My experience taught me that it was not sufficient to "fill in the blanks," I did best when I thought of something new, developed a requirement, stumbled onto some equipment improvement, corrected procedural discrepancies, then make a hero of the enlisted men who may have brought it to my attention. There's always better ways to accomplish anything. So, it began somewhere . . . thus, "Phase I."

I was born on July 11, 1937 in Louisville, Kentucky, four years into the murderous regime of NAZI thug Adoph Hitler, who had taken over Germany in January 1933.

My granddad, George Morris Worthington, was the International Oil Manager for IBM, which was endeavoring to entice world business into punch card technology. Because of his position he travelled the world continuously by air, sea, and rail. He and his wife lived in Pelham, New York, outside the city. On one visit in 1938, he carried home a couple of post cards from Berlin of the Fuhrer mounting his Mercedes convertible with a smiling Goebbels in the background. The photo was taken in front of the Rose Hotel, Wiesbaden. Lots of *Sieg Heil* arms outstretched. I suspect Wiesbaden (and the hotel) were later leveled by allied bombers. I mention the NAZIs because of the actual threat Germany presented to a witless Europe of the era. Having barely survived the "Great War," France and England were not anxious to sacrifice another generation. My first ten years of life was under threat—with the possible exclusion of 1945–1947. Then all hell broke loose with the lively competition with wartime ally Russia and Stalin. Events were worldwide: Berlin Airlift, France vs. Ho Chi Minh and the Viet Minh, and North Korea attacking the South. Always some existential challenge: U.S.S.R., Chinese Communists defeating Nationalists; Viet Cong, and the past ten-years-plus—9/11/91 to still wet ink on this page—radical Islamists chopping off heads.

One might more accurately figure the Islamic challenge from 1979 with the Iranian sacking of our embassy (without response).

Dad worked for IBM, which was also the company my granddad served with. We spent my first two years in Louisville, then went to Atlanta. In 1943–44 we lived in Pennsylvania, Jeanette, and Pittsburg, where my brother, William Junior, was born. Dad commissioned into the Navy in 1944, and we moved to Fort Pierce, Florida (which is where the original Navy Combat Demolition Units were formed). My first contact with sailors were PT boat crews.

The atomic bomb ended the Pacific War where Dad was training to lead landing craft onto the Home Island. Mom and us two boys moved to my paternal grandmother's town in Grapevine, Texas—back then a country town, today a bedroom suburb north of the Dallas-Ft. Worth Airport peak. My grandmother moved there following the passing of my grandfather. Late forties Texas was quiet—to me, anyway, age ten. High drama was climbing the China Berry tree in the driveway, catching lightening bugs in the summers, crayfish in the country streams, and year-long open season on horn frogs (and which we always treated with respect owing to it being the TCU mascot). The biggest North Texas threat to kids were potentially rattle snakes, which were common on Granddad's grapevine farm but happily scarce in town. The occasional scorpion could be discovered in the errand shoe; preventive measure meant shaking your shoes in the morning before thrusting your big toe into a cool boot!

I remember a new, post-World War II invention, the ballpoint pen that could write underwater. The Western Hardware Company was the closest time warp to today's WalMart. And all the rage for us kids were the Saturday movie matinees—Tarzan, Hopalong Cassidy, and Roy Rodgers were a few idols. We were not permitted to see Jane Russell movies, could watch pigs being emasculated or cows birthing. Texas boys, God bless 'em.

In late of 1948 we moved to Rockaway Park, Long Island, with Dad's post-Navy job in new '48—six-plus feet of snow fell on the entire region. Maybe it was less. I was only eleven and a great laugh with my Texas accent in Long Island barbershops. "I'd like a shot crow, please." (Translation: short crewcut)

Rockaway was a hoot! Ethically, it was chockful of Irish, Greeks, Jews, and some unidentified immigrants. In Rockaway, Mom sent me (an Episcopalian) to Catholic Saint Francis de Sales School; administered by the Sisters of St. Joseph, replete with black habits and peaked headdresses. (I still say Catholic prayers and cross myself before a sky dive, and "Hail Marys" work during an MRI). Rulers on the boys encouraged learning and vouchsafed morals. My fifth grade class was taught by Sister Helen. One time, classmate Tommy Scanlon leaned back over my pointer cleanly—and, okay, gently—across the back of his neck. Scanlon's surprised teeth bit clean through the candy. It was all the guys could do to keep from chortling out loud; my nose, to deflect complicity, went directly to the open page before me—with half a dog bone on it! Another, Sister Agnes—eighty-something, five feet tall—confronted big John Kirby, over five-eight and two hundred pounds. Sister Agnes demanded Kirby to bend over so she could slug him. His math performance improved.

One aspect of our East Coast occupation was spending summers with my grandmother at Lake Chautauqua in Western New York. She wintered in Pass-a-Grille, Florida, where I later visited during prep school vacations. Chautauqua is a summer arts community. Operas are performed in English, concerts every evening, day camp for kiddos, even lectures—everything a summering family could expect. Family restaurants are all over the place. And, if I remember, no public ale outlets inside the charter. And summer school tutors for algebra. And no saloons. I read my first books there, one of which was *Kon Tiki*. Many families come from Pittsburg. I remember young Larry Cummins of the diesel family; he played baseball catcher. Another friend was Ritz Academy. Small world.

Rockaway was a magic kingdom for us youngsters with its summer beach, body surfing, Playland amusement park blocks away in Far Rockaway, roofs for climbing, horseshoe crabs to attack in Jamaica Bay, and a bus ride to Brooklyn's St. George's Hotel with its indoor pool—great for Saturday ventures. St. Francis was a routine cornerstone in our behavior. Daily classes started with prayers and a weekly *novena* on Tuesday afternoons (in Latin in those days). A parish priest would come to class and deliver a short sermon once a week (in English). Homework was unknown as I recall—no twenty-pound book sacks in 1948. I can't recall tests either. We experimented with cigarettes. I'd walk a mile for a Camel and LSMFT (Lucky Strike Means Fine Tobacco). Remember all the movies—Bogie with a cigarette in every scene; John Wayne's signature flicking the butt away when it was time to "move 'em out?" Happily, the habit didn't stick! The girls were off-limits and fighting was rare.

We left Rockaway Beach for East Orange, New Jersey, in early summer 1951. Dad took a year's job in Ras Tanura, Saudi Arabia, with ARAMCO. Truth was he had a drinking problem and needed to get straightened out. He joined Alcoholics Anonymous (AA) and needed complete cultural sequestration to get it under control, which included complete abstinence—1951–1988, thirty-seven years sober. He was devoted to AA and would attend two and three meetings a week. I had "Friend of Bill" lodge members tell me at his funeral, "Your dad saved my life." How many sad stories do we recall of lives ruined? It still pains me to revisit the early years when he was drinking. During his sobriety he managed to get an MBA and Doctorate in Agricultural Business in Tucson's University of Arizona. He taught Statistics part time. But I'm getting ahead of myself.

The East Orange "deployment" experience was spotty. I still have a Clifford Scott 1952 yearbook. I wasn't making points with my Home Room and English teacher. Seems I couldn't connect with her (in English). But it wasn't to be an extensive relationship, my folks were moving to Tucson, Arizona, were Dad was to work for Hughes Aircraft Company. To ensure continuity, they decided to place me in a New England prep school—South Kent School, Connecticut—five miles south of Kent, the site of a similar prep school, Kent. (The 1923 South Kent founders, Sam Barlett and Dick Cuyler, were Kent graduates.)

The folks, with my sibling, went on to Tucson, Arizona. For four years I traversed the United States by rail with an occasional air transit—two days by rail, eight hours by plane. These weren't Pullman trips, although the diner car was available. It was sleeping on luggage. One Christmas vacation took me to Chicago's La Salle Street Station. Minsky's Burlesque was still operating. It was cold! I walked down Michigan Avenue's below zero and nearly froze Connecticut snow is "Norman Rockwell," Michigan snow is wind and frozen fingers!

For a few years Dad worked at Fort Huachuca. I was away at school; the family had quarters on Post, and later in Sierra Vista. I loved Tucson and the southern Apache Mountains of Ft. Huachuca and Sierra Vista. The countryside is magnificent. In Connecticut you are surrounded by trees and hills. The clouds drape your shoulders.

In Tucson you can see four weather systems over the 90-degree compass points of the local mountains. During summer we would swim in mountain creeks; July and August have rain every afternoon at four for at least thirty minutes—cleans out the air and drops the temperature ten degrees. It's beautiful. During my early active duty years, Tucson was my official home of record. I would work out of Davis-Monthan Air Force Base gym, and swim at the University of Arizona's 50-meter outdoor pool.

Come college selection at South Kent, I applied to Rice, Stanford, and Brown—in addition to applying to the U.S. Naval Academy. This academic adventure demands a new chapter. But a quick postscript of places and cultures that formed my early years: Louisville (go Cardinal!), Atlanta (during Pearl Harbor), Pittsburg, Florida (Daytona, Ft. Pierce, and New Smyrna), Grapevine, Rockaway Beach (where I learned to swim and body surf in the Atlantic). I lived through the NAZI-Fascist challenge, served in the active Navy from 1961 to 1992—and the proverbial Lion's Share of the Cold War—spent roughly forty-four months deployed to the far West serving in The Philippines, Vietnam, Japan, Malaysia, and Thailand. I will discuss more thoroughly.

Shot of me around 1943 in Jeanette, Pennsylvania. Dad had
commissioned in the Navy from Pittsburg. Note the Navy peacoat!

Postcard of *Der Fuhrer* in his Mercedes outside the Rose Hotel,
Wiesbaden, Germany, in 1938. Sent by my grandfather from
an IBM business trip. It was the Third Reich era into which my
generation was born.

CHAPTER 2

THE EDUCATION ROUTE SOUTH KENT SCHOOL, CONNECTICUT

I n the fall of 1952, as the family was moving to Tucson and Dad's new job, I reported into an all-boys South Kent School (SKS) (associated with the Episcopal Church) following an hour-and-a-half train ride from New York's Grand Central Station to South Kent crossing—SKS student drop-off. It was September 24, 1952. I met a couple of the "old boys" on the train singing to the "Last Chance" snack purveyor:

> "Don't cry, Last Chance, we'll buy your Coca-Colas,
> Don't cry, Last Chance, we'll buy your pencils, too…
> Don't cry, Last Chance, take off those dark blue glasses
> Hello Mother, I knew it was you."

By the time we arrived I was cold and hungry and thankful when a school "Master" scooped us all up just as the light was fading on a hilly landscape challenged by strange shadows and lonesome crows catching the last rays of the Indian Summer sun. A five-minute bus ride up the South Kent hill—a serious hill, challenging during snowy days. The school was founded on an English "Public School" model. Classes are called forms; freshmen are third formers; second year sophomores are fourth, fifth, and sixth, etc. Coats and ties were daily dress—lace up shoes, loafers not permitted—spawning lots of competition for English Regimental ties and cordovan shoes. Ah, the hours spent spit-shining for the competition; a pair of Brook's Brothers cord bluchers cost $35, over $600 today. All the boys were label conscious.

The South Kent School academic year is divided into fall, winter, and in spring semesters; classes are held Monday through Saturday noon. "Wake up" was 0645; breakfast was 0715 sharp—late arrivals got to run the mile down to the tracks and back, a fifteen-minute jaunt in coat and tie, nobody ran fast so as not to break a sweat. Breakfast was oatmeal or cream of wheat with muffins and hot tea. Morning assembly—ninety-five students—was 0800 with announcements and an occasional harangue by the Head Master. Classes began at 0815 and ran until 1:00 PM; lunch followed at 1:15 PM. A sole afternoon class went from 2:00 to 3:00 PM. Sports at 3:30 to 5:30 (or so). Showers and a fifteen-minute chapel session were followed by dinner at 6:30 PM; evening Study Hall or in-room study for upper classes started at 7:45 PM and ran to 9:00 PM; lights out at 10:00 PM. Saturday afternoons were reserved for sports. Sunday: 10:00 AM Episcopalian church ceremony and a hefty Sunday lunch around 12:30 PM. Afternoon, free time to catch up on courses.

Saturday evening meal was "formal." That meant suits with vests and candlelit tables. After desert the Headmaster would deliver a speech, lecture, sermon. Many tales were of the early years after school founding in 1923, early football games and particular athletic standouts. Many had moral overtones of life in the big city—from a New England perspective. It was a very provincial outlook, but that's what the parents were paying for. One tidbit was the fact that in the twenties, thirties, and forties all businessmen wore hats! (It was before "Monty Python, The Meaning of Life.") I don't recall anybody paying much attention to 1930s sartorial splendor on Madison Avenue.

SKS offered only football in the fall. Everybody suited up on three age-grouped skills, much Like Pop Warner youth football is formed today. Better skilled players advanced to a higher team. My recall dates from years 1952–1956. Since then, sixty-three years ago, the school got into basketball and several grads are playing in the NBA.

SKS colors are red and black. The teams are nicknamed "Cardinals." Our football uniforms in those days reflected the twenties—old leather helmets with no face guards, one or two Ridels. Concussions back then were handled like bruises unless you were knocked out. Black electric tape was used to take up slack in the legs—we were all skinny. Few were accomplished. We played with other New England prep schools—Kent, Gunnery, Salisbury, Canterbury, Taft among them. Following the game and showers, both teams were served hot chocolate and brownies in clubby "common rooms." The SKS common room—empty except for window benches and rows of former students reminding one like an early century Yale yearbook. It was very chummy and sportsmanlike—preparing the future Wall Street barons. My Sixth Form (senior) football experience wasn't particularly rewarding; we didn't win a game the entire season. I'm still wondering what I learned from that experience. (Things later worked better in the pool!)

Winter was full contact ice hockey. I couldn't skate when winter arrived around Connecticut mid-November—not so much snow but chilly temperatures. It took three weeks for the pond to freeze over. But I learned sharp skates and the use of folded *New York Times* for shin pads, held firm by that football electric tape. The teams were formed on skill and age. The best skaters were New England kids. We skated on Hatch Pond, a three-quarter mile lake that on colder periods formed black ice, fifteen inches of the hardest ice. That soft mush on indoor rinks is much slower than thick black ice. And your skates need be extremely sharp. On clear snowless days, we could skate the entire length of the pond passing pucks back and forth. The pond had rinks cut out which were floated above the rest of the ice by several inches. Then it was flooded for a smooth surface. The school had two other outdoor rinks closer to the dorms but with the white ice. A couple of days during winter the Headmaster would stand up at breakfast and announce a "skating day"—full up no class! We'd be down at Hatch by 8:30 and rip off three hours of skating. Back for lunch then back down. Fatigue never entered the equation. Of course, the sun went down around 4:30 so we were monitored by nature. No problem sleeping after skate day!

In spring there were three sports available—baseball, crew, or tennis. I played two years of baseball, third Base; couldn't hit, though—later determined poor depth perception. I went out for crew and rowed bow in "fours"—our shells were four rowers; "eights" would overpower the pond. In summary, sports were fun at SKS. I was to learn later playing freshman football at Brown that college sports were more demanding.

Class leadership was the order of the day at South Kent. The first form (seniors) ran the school self-help jobs program. The student leaders were called "prefects." Three prefects from the incoming sixth formers were picked before the school year by the Headmaster—a senior prefect and two "vice prefects." My roommate of three years, Tom Allan, was senior prefect. I was one of the lesser knights. All the kids had janitorial jobs—sweeping, dish washing, washroom cleaning, and the like. Jobs were done between breakfast and morning assembly. Sixth formers were the job inspectors. Poor performance was rewarded with extra "hours." Extra doing some manual exercise like sweeping leaves in fall. A sixth form "sheriff" was in charge of the work gang. The discipline at South Kent was pretty taut, and time at SKS was allotted for every event. Weekly entertainment was sports and a 1940s vintage rerun Saturday night after the candlelit evening dinner.

Brown, Providence, R.I.

Sometime in the spring of 1956, I got notice that I had been accepted by Brown. My course work included Latin and French (two years each), Algebra 2, Geometry, English, History, Religion, and Physics. I was probably a "3.0" student, the only class that really stuck was French, which I took at Brown and later at the Naval Academy. It was book French, add the proper verb endings and memorize the rest. Little attention was spent on actually speaking the language—neither at the Roslyn State Department total immersion course in French—gave me headaches!

I reported to Providence, a delightful city—as is Newport where I did a Navy course later. But Brown was on the list for the moment. Freshmen were requested to come in a week before the university reassembled to start the 1956–57 academic year. I was assigned to Maxie Hall, an all-class/all-male dormitory. (Brown shared classes with Pembroke; my lit class had three Pembroke students.) I signed up for classes, one of which was a math class that I swear I never understood a word the professor was talking about. He might as well been speaking "Martian" with Star Wars robot R2-D2, which didn't exist then.

Freshmen reported in a week before the upper three classes to learn the grounds, learn the songs, cheers, and general orientation. The evenings were sprinkled with "introduction to beer" parties, normally in the dorm basements. Since I was planning going out for freshman football, I stayed off keg, which made it difficult to abide the inevitable drunks. One night I noticed an empty six pack of Buds left on the dorm porch. I figured it an oversight and picked it up, only to see the same carelessness the next night. At South Kent we were taught to take care of your neighborhood and police up trash. That "careless" example unfortunately seemed to spillover into other aspects of Brown community, like sparse attendance at varsity football rallies.

Classes convened and the academic crunch begun. I signed up for contract NROTC, i.e., no Fiscal scholarship support. I was already on the Naval Reserve list as a Seaman Recruit, having enlisted after my eighteenth birthday and a two-week introduction to Boot Camp in San Diego in the summer 1955. (I still have my pocket notebook from Boot Camp lectures on ships, seamanship, General Orders, chain of command, UCMJ, etc.) In the middle weekend of the two weeks we were authorized Saturday afternoon "liberty" in downtown San Diego. What a difference in skyline between 1955 and today's billed "America's Finest City." Back then, the tallest building was the El Cortez Hotel. Downtown was "Sailorville," collection of beer bars, Army-Navy stores, movie houses, and Shore Patrol squads keeping peace. We grabbed burgers and went to a John Wayne movie. We got back to base at eight, well in time for taps. The experience was a toot, did not influence my Brown Navy ROTC status, but several years on, in 1963, my enlisted service impacted my base pay entry date from commissioning in 1961 to 1959—a couple thousand dollars that paid for a trip to Europe on leave.

I got back to South Kent in September 1955 for my sixth (senior) form year. For my college applications I had three sports and a student council membership to recommend me. Rice and Stanford declined the offer; Brown accepted.

At Brown, I went out for freshman football. It was much more demanding experience than SKS. Suffice it to say, I was terrible. I tried out for tight end, didn't matter what position I might have opted for; I was terrible. Not lacking courage—saw stars on every tackle (we played both sides of the ball then). It was a tough fall! But some light emerged. Out last evening of practice was under lights at 5:30 (Rhode Island in November). The very next day, I went over to the pool and reported to the swim coach, Joe Watmough. And my life changed, albeit unknown too me at the time. The pool lights were brilliant. The temperature was "Florida!" Guys were laughing. No "grrrrs" or grunts evident. Guys called the coach Joe, not *Mein Furhrer.* Guys were laughing, but I said that; the culture was totally "180" from the football team. But, in fairness, the sports are totally different.

I had a good experience swimming at Brown on the freshman team. No balls to drop, a lane line to guide the course, a cross at the end to announce time to turn . . . Then the life-changer—I told coach Joe that I still wanted to go to the Naval Academy. Turns out, Watmough had coached the Academy coach at the time,

John Higgins, at the Rhode Island Olneyville Boys Club to the 1936 Berlin Olympics. Higgins was eighteen at those games; he later went to Michigan where he was a perennial All America and American record holder.

Fast forward to summer 1957. I'm home in Tucson swimming for the local YMCA when in mid-June I received an invitation from the U.S. Naval Academy to report on July 1, 1957, for swearing in as part of the Class of 1961. About that same time I got an invitation from Brown to come back for early varsity football training. What a marvelous decision—I picked Navy. Turns out Joe Watmough phoned John Higgins and advised him of my efforts a year earlier to get to Crab Town. (Many years later, in my last active assignment, I heard from a former Academy Acceptance Board president that applicants not making in on the first cut were 100 percent assured to get an offer after a year in college. I slough it off as an athletic scholarship for swimming.)

Annapolis, Maryland

The United States Naval Academy: four years of turmoil. To start with, in prep school, the boys were exhorted to take interest in school society, to care for your environment, and help each other. At Brown, in the early to mid-fifties the cultural mantel evident in the Ivy League was one of bemused nonchalance. At USNA, it was a Plebe "rate" to care about your teams and exhibit emotion—*go navy, beat army!*

Plebe Summer started July 1 with swearing in at Memorial Hall, Bancroft Hall. Then a "Uniform Party." Party—a Navy term for a work team, e.g., five-man working party, etc. Our Uniform Party consisted of over 1,200 newly signed on fourth class Midshipmen.

Full complement of uniforms would take several days getting fitted for white work gear, formal blues, caps and hats (a difference). We kept our own shaving kits and toothbrushes. Once outfitted, we were rather gently initiated to Naval Academy lore; more rigorous brass scrubbing, bracing up, finning out palms, squaring to turns, "eyes in the boat," "running" by foremost second class (juniors), all meals eaten on the edge of your chair, head and eyes "in the boat"—twentieth century slavery in action—gross memorization of upper class questions, and tasks to be completed by the next meal . . . on top of academics, sports, personal uniform prep, etc.

First of all, one had to remember the question/task . . . and who asked it! But I'm getting ahead of myself; to end the two-month summer adventure, we learned how to fire the M-1, sail a knockout, spit shine shoes, block a Navy flat had, fold clothes, make a bed, march, workout for fitness events, e.g., physical testing (Plebe Summer I was number 2, an eventual teammate was first), manual of arms, nautical terminology, memorization of Navy songs and competing universities' fight songs. "A cheer, a cheer for old Notre Dame, wake up the echoes shouting her name . . ."

Truth be known, Plebe Summer was informative, entertaining, and basic teenage fun. The hardest part was learning academic lore—Navy history, the Academy "Yard," all the buildings' names, and something about the naval officers whose names they boasted. We had two months of Plebe Summer to digest the nooks and crannies of the Naval Academy and the Annapolis Main Street. The quaint town in 1957 was straight out of "Porgy and Bess," as I remember it. Few of us had any relationship with the downtown harbor bars and yachting watering holes. Midshipmen were forbidden alcohol within thirty miles (or was it fifty?) And Annapolis had one two-lane, state highway to the District of Columbia and the same to Baltimore. At mid-century both those east coast cities were holdovers from the nineteenth century. It's my opinion that Baltimore had a harbour renaissance of redevelopment, which included building a football stadium. Hearsay rumor has it European city fathers asked the Baltimore government how they did it. Annapolis, along with the State Seat, has become another bedroom lodging for Washington Federal workers. Annapolis is arguably the sailing capitol of the world—used to be Newport, R.I. Annapolis enjoys a longer season. When I was at the Academy (1957–61), downtown was rarely a destination; most went out to the "drag houses," (bed and breakfast) private hostels for young ladies—most often chaperoned by the lady of the house guarding against dating hanky-panky. Then there was the Saturday evening "Midnight Squadron," last Mids on liberty racing back to beat the clock and avoid being put on report for lateness. Whew! Safely in Bancroft Hall at the stroke of midnight.

Racing forward in time with my attendance at Attaché School, summer 1974, in preparation for assignment to Cambodia. I would venture to Annapolis on weekends; remarkable restoration was undertaken on the Annapolis waterfront—new bars and restaurants predominated, most all worthwhile. Five years later, as a student at National War College (1978–79), we routinely visited Annapolis and my favorite joint was McGarvey's Bar and Grill, owned by former Air Force and Eastern Airlines pilot Mike Ashford—herewith a flagrant plug: try the steamed mussels and black bean soup.

But Plebe Year was a grind. Classes—have to pass them all! Plebe "rates," and working out for the sports team—swimming in my case, years before goggles and all turns were hand-touch.

I mentioned earlier the cultural difference between the nonchalance of the Ivy League and the Gung Ho culture of the Naval Academy (and I presume the other service academies). Plebes and upper classes were committed to sports enthusiasm—it was a "Plebe Rate" (must do pressure) to support the teams. Plebes were responsible for memorizing all coaches and weekend sports events in The Yard. If at a meal a Plebe did not know the answer to a question, the correct response is, "I'll find out, Sir," no "I don't knows." The first challenge for the Plebe is to remember the question! Escalation point because all hell unloads of the forgetful Plebe. I cannot emphasize the stress placed on memorization at USNA. The U.S. Navy is equipment oriented. Operating at sea with other ships information requires a quick uptake on ship disposition (boilers on line, superheat, in-line or cross-connected, communications, and tactical situation—on, above, below the surface, and out to and beyond the horizon). The ability to take on massive dumps of information requires training and practice. (It helped in class, too! Somehow, remembering what the boss said counts across the board in any occupation.)

I recall one mythological gesture as we marched to final exams. Midshipmen would throw pennies at the courtyard statue of the Native American Tecumseh. I threw growth mutual funds. (Jus' kidding!) Plebe year wound up with the graduation of the class of 1958 and Plebes putting a white mid-cap on top of greased up Herndon Monument. Plebe year over. Whoopee!

Plebe Cruise—mine was aboard the helicopter carrier USS Lake Champlain, an anti-submarine ship. New "youngsters" (sophomores) became familiar with shipboard systems from an enlisted point of view. Ports visited were Vigo, Spain, where we went to a cocktail party attended by Juan Carlos, the future king (appointed by Franco). In our shore excursions to downtown Vigo bars, we learned not all Spaniards were happy with the dictator. The Spanish dining hours came as a shock. The young ladies of Spain came to the club around

5:00 PM, left at 6:60 –7:00 PM, and returned around 9:00 PM—by which time we were all "shit faced." Zero romance resulted.

Next port of call, Copenhagen, Denmark. Spent all our time at Tivoli Garden, a magnificent pre-Disneyland experience—shows, rides, mixer opportunities, great Carlsberg beer, great food; strawberries as big as your fist, sagging table boards, with decent prices too! Floating electric boats to drive around the bayou with a humorous sign on the dashboard: "Fart," Yuk, yuk . . . meaning "go." Copenhagen left a great feeling among us Mids that July 1958.

Final stop, Edinburgh, Scotland. We attacked downtown like barbarians. Fortunately, United Kingdom bar hours confused us. We somehow ended up in the countryside at a Scottish sing-along at long tables laden with beer. We couldn't understand a word of the Scottish brogue, even with beer—Hoot Mon! But it was fun. Norfolk was the terminal before post-cruise departure on one month summer leave. For me back to Arizona; after Labor Day, back to the fall grind. Third Class Youngsters were not permitted to run Plebes.

For varsity athletes it was regroup drills to prepare for the upcoming 1958–59 season. Now on the varsity swim team, I concentrated on the butterfly—100 and 200 yard distances. The hundred-yard fly was a minute sprint; the two-hundred was an ordeal beyond repentance—a lonely two-minute plus trial by drowning. When I first began the stroke, I was lucky if my wrists broke the water on the final eighth lap. I felt in need of a heart message afterward. But you learn . . . slowly, it became psychologically mind-over-matter. The following years and twenty-year career in Masters Swimming made it durable. The tactical trick was to stay as flat as possible, keep the overall body undulation associated with butterfly stabilized. I was the fly leg of our 400-yard medley relay team. In winter/early spring we go lucky and made the top ten earning All America status for 1959. That was my last hoorah in the hundred because a faster California kid (Dick Cheery) kicked my butt. I still held on to the 200 for two more years (and Naval Academy records).

Having broached the last two years, Second Class year was generally the one that historically ruined guys' eyes—obviating flight school. Chockablock schedule. The summer before "Secundo" year was spent with the Marines and Flight school Marines in Little Creek and air at Pensacola. First Class year seemed a bit more tranquil—courses seemed less demanding, but that might be illusory. It was more hard core Navy subjects on how machinery worked. Of course there was a big paper due, which challenged "see spot run." The summer before was a fleet assignment to a destroyer, USS DuPont, with the Sixth Fleet in the Mediterranean. We had port calls in Trieste and Rapallo (both Italy)—two only this cruise.

First Class (senior) year was relatively light compared to the one just finished. No free rides, but seemingly a more pressure-free schedule. My penchant for procrastinating had not yet been conquered. Finals were highlighted by all-nighters—page one, who wrote the textbook, preface, chapter layout, chapter one ... until morning reveille bell—breakfast, throw the pennies ("Growth Mutual Fund") at Tecumseh, stay the entire three hours, stop by the chapel on the way to lunch ... hope for the best ... I made it to graduation, June 7, 1961, with President Kennedy speaking, and with orders in hand I shoved off in my new TR-3 two-place Triumph sport car. (Cost spring 1961 at $2,400!) I headed out to Sierra Vista, Arizona. Dad still at Huachuca. (They had come to graduation and flew home. I made stops on the way with various friends.) I was to report in to my command by July 15, then in overhaul at Long Beach; back to San Diego early September. And my active duty life began.

THE EDUCATION ROUTE PICTURES

Welcome to South Kent School (SKS), South Kent, Connecticut. The school on the hill with a mott at that time, "Pigtail Against the World." Well, maybe that's a big bite. Essentially aligned with the Protestant Episcopal Church, the school philosophy and basic culture was self-help, personal responsibility, and singleness of purpose—all instilled over four years.

Old roommate, Tom Allan, and I at an annual
school reunion (looks like 1994).

My 1956 graduation portrait for the yearbook.

Following my second year at South Kent, I enlisted
in the Naval Reserve as a Seaman Recruit. My Father
swore me in. Date of enlistment was July 25, 1955 (the
year Naval Academy Quarterback George Welsh—triple
option magician—graduated!).

SKS is a small Connecticut College Preparatory school. Sixteen in my 1956 graduating class. I'm first row, third from the right. White Bucks were in vogue even in winter.

Senior (Sixth Form) "First" Team, not "Varsity." The
"Old Man," Headmaster, Sam Bartlett, hated the word.
I'm front row second from right. My roommate, Tom
Allan (No. 50), was Team co-Captain and Head Prefect.

1957 NAVY PLEBE

Seaman Recruit George Worthington, eighteen years old, back
from two weeks "boot" training at the Naval Training Command,
San Diego. Years later, as an admiral, I would deliver a graduation
speech to a graduating class. My Navy career went from initial
summer camp to NROTC at Brown University, to the U.S. naval
Academy. "Runnin' with Frogs" would come later.

Another uniform, formal Navy summer whites.
Picture second ("Youngster") year.

Sports. The swim team, which got me into the Naval Academy; our 4x100 Medley Relay Team. Left to right: Kurt Norfleet (freestyle), me (butterfly), Pat Taft (breaststroke), Arnie Kleban (backstroke). We made the 1959 All America Team (eked ninth in the nation).

CHAPTER 3

ACTIVE DUTY: FIRST ASSIGNMENTS

Thus ended my Phase I on June 7, 1961, and Phase II began on June 8, 1961, when I set out for San Diego—Long Beach, actually—via several stops cross-country to visit friends and relatives, about ten days or so. I reported into USS HALSEY POWELL (DD-686) late July . . . to enjoy a month in a shipyard. An orchestral cacophony of sawing, banging, grinding, sanding, clanking, pounding, whining—sounds of sailors working! All I knew of shipboard existence was collected from summer cruises. It was like the first days on a new sports team. I was assigned to the Operations Department which included Combat Information Center, Communications, and Electronics Divisions. I was given Electronics as the EMO (Electronics Material Officer). What did I know about "Comm/ET?" Within six months I was assigned as the Registered Publications System (RPS) control officer, where your life depends on every single page of the crypto code account. Every quarter an audit is conducted by two assigned officers after which lapsed or expired code documents are incinerated. Side arms accompanied two officers (always me) charged with burning the booklets and signed off each time. I was also charged with the top secret cryptographic encoding systems, about which read the book on "enigma."

We refloated from dry dock and returned to rural San Diego early September. In 1961, the San Diego skyline was singularly outlined with the 1927 El Cortez Hotel atop a hill of the same name, right next to Balboa Park, a grand old lady since refurbished for condos. The rest of the city was maybe a half-dozen stories "about as high as a building ought to go . . ." according to Oklahoma. Vietnam changed all that. San Diego is beginning to resemble Hong Kong with high-rise office space.

We were berthed at the 31nd Street Naval Surface Station. Wives were taxied to Long Beach to retrieve vehicles; bachelors had to convoy back. Families got quarters allowances; bachelors got nothing. Guys would chip in for "snake ranches" in San Diego's Mission Bay and Virginia Beach on the East Coast. I recall the dress code at the time was coat and tie for most evenings. Vietnam relaxed dress codes a lot; the dress standards took ten years to really loosen up. I feel the first death knell was Officers' Clubs. On the West Coast, sixties Friday nights at the Marine Corps Recruit Depot Officers Club served over a thousand patrons from six to midnight. Sunday afternoons were hot starting back in 1964; on the North Island Air Station beach, guys would come in swimsuits for pitchers of beer between 4:00 PM and 6:00 PM, at which bewitching it closed. People would run home to shower and post at the Mexican Village. Late sixties, the Mission Beach watering holes were the Beach Comer and the Pennant—side by side and still going strong. Sociological issues still bother the services, that is, women in combat, compensation, health care (universal!), etc. The O-Clubs, first appendages to go, were followed by retiree dental care. Commissaries are under scrutiny now . . . to the glee of commercial grocery stores and cut-rate membership outlets. General revision of military benefits are under scrutiny by Congress, for example, the twenty-year retirement formula will probably be the first to relax. Stay tuned. I suspect great change will be of negative career impact on service beyond the first two enlistments. And, dare it be said, sequestration is overtaxing the force—expected to do more with less.

Post shipyard availability requires reformation of crews and combat teams—weapons instruction and employment, emergency casualty control teams; fire and battle damage repair, and overall crew readiness for sea. Refresher training is conducted on each coast, San Diego and Norfolk—actually, Guantanamo Bay (GITMO), Cuba. It lasts six weeks of grueling drills and at-sea performance exercises. Its exacerbating team building construction, creating a ship family of confidence and professionalism, which becomes more competent throughout the follow-on overseas deployment. Both coasts have shore-based schools for combat teams and qualifying test cadres, the "Black Hatters." The GITMO experience is time away from homeport (families). San Diego combined local area employment and naval gunfire drills at San Clemente Island; some family relief. A great shipboard "whew!" On that last Friday followed by an all hands beach party, rain or shine!

Powell's REFTRA lasted to mid-October, followed by a week of in-port maintenance and upkeep—a gentle stand-down from the rigorous training. We were then ready for local fleet exercises and normal training in home waters, which in those days meant out Monday back Friday—training not affordable today. The guy with weekend duty got Friday night off then reported for duty

Saturday 0800; underway Monday morning. My first Christmas holiday season afforded me a "close and personal" relationship with the Uniform Code of Military Justice (UCMJ). I was appointed government prosecuting officer for a Special Courts Martial, which system was replaced sometime later to 1961; lawyers are required today. Christmas Eve 1961 was spent with nose deep into the UCMJ bible—court procedures, proof, evidence, witnesses, log records, etc. I was an Ensign; the President of the Court, a Lieutenant (the Ops Officer). The accused was found guilty. Duh! He was AWOL two weeks—leave documentation and date of return. "Desertion" starts at thirty days. Welcome to the Navy!

Then, after a more-or-less tranquil spring, we got orders assigning Powell to Joint Task Force EIGHT for Operation DOMINIC, the 1962 nuclear tests conducted north of Christmas Island in the Pacific, south of Hawaii. Security was tight. Our mission—and Destroyer Squadron (DESRON) SEVEN ships—was to patrol the outward approaches to the test sites. No photographic gear was permitted. Reprinted here, we signed the following:

"16 July 1962

I have been informed of and understand the following facts concerning the releast of Information about OPERATION DOMINIC:

A. There will be no military public issuance of release on return of units of personnel to their home stations.
B. The following may be stated in answer to query: "HALSEY POWELL has returned after serving

with JTF-8 in Operation Dominic, the nuclear test
program in the Pacific."

C. No request for interviews of personnel will be granted.

D. No photographs of personnel or equipment will
be released."

Signed by me and the Executive Officer. Entire crew
signed one. Got our attention—Ho Hum . . .

The transit to Pearl Harbor was remembered for its rough (Pacific—
calm waters?) passage a day out of San Diego. Six destroyers in
formation for the normally five-day transit at sixteen knots. We
endured three days of Sea State 4! Waves higher than the bridge.
We could see the guide ship only on the crest of a wave. Eating was
impossible—water and saltines! A coffee pot couldn't stay upright.
I tied my arm into my bunk at night with my web belt to keep from
falling out! Great weight control plan . . . Zero maintenance work
was done. Limited underway drills could be done. The Combat
Information Center guys kept us on station; signal flags were
too wet to fly—who could see them, anyway? We kept too radio
bands up. "Fleet Common" on AM, "Pri-Tac" on FM, neither used
much. It was a baptism of barf . . . great weight control plan! But
I said that. A day out of Hawaii, the sun came out. We picked up
the birds about twenty-five miles out, gulls mostly. On occasion
seafarers will catch dolphins, flying fish, gulls, and the "Ancient
Mariner's" albatross.

My first visit to Hawaii, before the popular TV show "Hawaii
Five-O." I was extremely lucky to have the weekend free from duty.
I booked a room in the Ala Moana Hotel, on the far end of Waikiki
and on the water. The most alluring draw, I was to happily learn, was

its magnificent breakfast. For a famished, skinny Navy guy after four days on starvation rations, it was wonderful—and, too, it followed a filet mignon steak the night before at Chuck's, one of the early stake/serve-yourself-salad joints soon to make a profitable profile on the mainland. And the basic challenge of our Pearl Harbor berth was to get Powell ready for extended at-sea periods in a high humid climate. For our communications team, the drill was to rig a low frequency antenna to receive LF traffic from fleet headquarters in Hawaii. This baby reached from the masthead to the stern. Long range communications, then, relied on Morse code—dit-dit-dah-dit-dit. Radiomen could identify each other by the touch of their "fists." Our main LF radio was tagged "TBL," a behemoth in Radio Central. Happily, it worked, and my 250-pound Chief Radioman garnered a lot of credit. (His expertise was acknowledged; he'd never survive the weight-conscious service today.)

Security proscriptions still obtain. So what? We were never cut into the technical specs of the tests anyway; just keep ships out of the blast area, a 25-mile radius from detonation. I saw two test explosions at that 25-mile range. We were "Circle William" closure (totally secured) on detonation and required to remain inside for sixty seconds. Upon exiting, it was "high noon" brilliance for 360 degrees—brighter than Death Valley in August. Then a slow, improvised dusk descended on the entire region, leaving a smoldering, angry magenta burning light in the sky. Itself luminous like a fireplace coal. The burn lasted several hours. We all joke about how we might glow in the dark.

Back and forth for two months, sharing patrol duties with the other destroyers. Between at-sea times we were able to enjoy Hawaii, and the sailors could concentrate on rating exams. Upkeep rites were facilitated by the proximity of the Pearl Harbor shipyard. If a system had trouble, "tech-rep" support was available. Our Comm-ET gang were no problems. The base recreation facilities were (and are) outstanding. The only thing lacking for a portion of the crew were the families. As often in Navy life, and all services, separation is a fact of life, in my opinion, ignored by Congress when it comes to benefits.

Staying fit at sea—I had a plan. As a former college swimmer—three-year letterman at USNA—I was a fitness fanatic. Holding onto a ship during rough weather is a workout of its own. During the placid steaming seas of the South Pacific, a more active routine was required to get the blood moving. In swim competition, carried over from track, interval training sets remains rigorous to develop physical proficiency. My shipboard workout, which I have used on subsequent ships, involved push-ups and chins; legs were strengthened by squats and leg levers. My push-ups were performed by pumping out twenty-five every minute. Twenty-five would take approximately twenty-five to thirty seconds to do; hop up, shake arms, deep breathe, and drop down for another set. I got up to 500 push-ups—breathing hard, sweating the heat, jumping around gently to decompress. Worked great; and I would do this set every other day, depending on ship schedule and watch routines. I was able to stay in relatively good condition, and added shore and pool workouts when back at Pearl. Of course, you don't have to start out with twenty-five; try twenty or whatever number works to keep the minute frequency.

We were back in San Diego late August 1962, ready to start training for a forthcoming Western Pacific (WESTPAC) deployment. I note the date, because at the Base Theater the first James Bond flick, "Doctor NO," had opened. I didn't bother, thinking it a "C" level bore. One item accrued from my Christmas Island workout drill. Back home the squadron decided to sponsor an "Ironman," although I'm not certain how much real interest a community of surface sailors gave it.

Preparation for overseas movement involves getting up to speed on the Combatant Commander Instructions and forward numbered fleet operating regulations—not hard, but requiring of some wardroom intensity to ensure ship's bill (working instructions) were in line with forward requirements. Noteworthy of this period in Navy modernization were (1) the automation of communications cryptology and (2) periodic maintenance of equipment and documentation (PQMS)—Personal Qualification and Maintenance System (if memory serves). Both were cultural adaptations. The communications arrangement meant synchronizing transmissions with uniform crypto systems. It eliminated the Morse code tap requirement for radiomen. System maintenance—preventive maintenance—flew in the face of a culture that believed, "if it ain't broke, don't fix it." Taking a working pump off line to document oiling took a generation to instill. On the officer level, who was to be the Czar to implement enforcement? Started out with executive officers made that job near impossible . . . melding haircuts and discipline with PMS implementation. Adaptation was a long and lonely transition.

One day in March 1963, my ship to orders from Commander Cruiser Destroyer Flotilla SEVEN to have me report for interview with the Commander, then Rear Admiral Francis Boyle, a World War II Navy Cross submariner who sank a Japanese cruiser. My C.O. knew the drill, it was to interview for Aide and Flag Lieutenant. I "greased up" with haircut, starched shirt, and spit shine—we had shoulder board summer khakis then—and reported to the Command Flag Lieutenant, a 1955 Naval Academy grad; Boyle was Class of 1933. I met the roly-poly admiral in his quarters—forgot which ship, a missile destroyer? I explained to him how I was prepping for a SEVENTH FLEET deployment with the Flotilla in June, that I was seeking to "fleet up" to Operations Officer, that I would miss vital shipboard experience, blah, blah, etc. Boyle said cut the crap and good job selling the Navy, check in with the Flag Lieutenant for a "Loafer's Loop (aiguillette)," and cut orders. I sadly reported back to Powell and admitted to failure to convince. Of course, competition among the junior officers wasn't misplaced.

I detached from Powell and reported into COMCRUDESFLOT SEVEN the same week, no leave. The Flat Lieutenant gave me a "loop" and the San Diego phone book, all needed for the job, plus learning all the Commanding Officers in the Flotilla. A month later the admiral volunteered me to compete in the Naval Pentathlon Championship in Karlskrona, Sweden, sponsored by the Council International de Sport Militaire (CISM), International Military Sport Council. In the meantime, I started working out, and we deployed late August. Another weekend in my beloved Hawaii— another steak at Chuck's. We left for Midway where I detached, and made my way back to San Diego to report in the Underwater Demolition Team TWELVE on July 1 for workout and trials for the U.S. "Sea Week" CISM team. I think about twenty UDT guys were trying out—and one Marine, 1st LT. Gordy Collet, former NAAA champion breaststroker at the University of Oklahoma. Lieutenant Ted Lyon was UDT-12 Operations Officer in charge of CISM charges. Collet and I were the only Fleet entries. Chief Petty Officer Don Rose, who had participated in the previous year's CISM, was pentathlon coach. We started working out, 0800-1600 daily—grueling, close to SEAL basic training. We had a first-time after two weeks; I won. Two more weeks of training to semi-final cuts. A dozen were taken back to Little Creek for All Navy Pentathlon

Championships from which the final team was chosen. I won. All set for late August departure.

Travel excursion. San Diego to London, London to Copenhagen to Malmo to Karlskrona. The Scandinavian teams were masters of the pentathlon, which consisted of five "penta" events—obstacle course, swimming obstacle course, seamanship event, swimming lifesaving, and cross-country amphibian event—all on time, lowest score wins—from top down: (1) Sweden (82 pts), (2) Norway (123 pts), (3) USA (196.5 pts), (4) Netherlands (211.5), (5) Greece (279.5 pts), (6) Turkey (294 pts), (7) Italy (318.5 pts), (8) Belgium (370 pts), (9) France (408 pts). I was first American, ninth overall, Sweden took four of the first five places, Norway second four, us 9th and 10th (Collet). As we got better over time from 1963, the U.S. medal count increased. I was destined to be a team leader for two more CISM championships—to Brazil and Den Helder, Holland; we won both. All was fine with the CISM world until 9/11. And more, the annual Naval Special Warfare Fourth of July demonstrations have been curtailed. Frogmen (SEALs) are doing multiple deployments overseas, often with six months break or maybe a year. (It happened with my son.) But I'm writing now about 1963. I got questioned in Oslo on our way home about our early presence in Vietnam. 1963 Vietnam . . . where's that? (I was soon to learn and spent forty-four months in and out of the Far East.)

On my way home from Sweden, the Navy Personnel officer, a Commander, invited me to stick around another month for the CISM swimming championship which was scheduled to be held in Barcelona, Spain, in early October. He indicated a message would go to my command for approval. What the heck, another month or so. Admiral Boyle approved, and I was back in the pool. Whew! No more obstacle course, cross-country running, seamanship rowing with anchors. Loosen up the swim muscles—totally different conditioning. The CISM swimming team seemed to be all-service make-up, not strictly Navy Frogmen. I recognized many of the competitors from my Naval Academy competition days—Ivy League sprinters, mostly from Yale and Princeton. All great guys and nobody in former NCAA condition, so I wasn't alone. The final team never worked out together; it was marry up at Dulles Airport and deploy to Spain. I loved it. What a great city. Barcelona took care of breakfast and lunch; we did our own dinners. I was expecting Mexican food—not. It is very continental. Great Mediterranean seafood and escargot. I won't say it was the best training diet. I don't even remember the results. It was a cultural exchange. Finally got back to COMCRUDESFLOT SEVEN late October 1963, just as things were heating up in Indochina. We steamed over to Vietnamese waters to familiarize the sailors and crews with the region. We loitered two weeks up and down the coast. This was several months before the summer 1964 Tonkin Gulf dust-up occurred.

Early in November, Rear Admiral Boyle was relieved by World War II Destroyerman Rear Admiral Ed Miller, a destroyer Navy Cross winner. Our time in Subic Bay was nearing its term. We finished up our WESTPAC deployment and headed home. We were two days west of Pearl Harbor when we received word of President Kennedy's assassination. The entire ship was thunderstruck! Who could not like and admire JFK? And he was a wartime Navyman; remember, 1963 was only two decades from WW II, and all the U.S. senior fleet flag slots were filled by "War Two" vets—attributing, perhaps, to an outdated strategy approach to Vietnam (an argument for later). Okay, get the personality crap out of the way; what recent politician is now graced with as much humor and warmth as John

Kennedy and his young family—maybe Reagan, except for the youngsters? A dark shadow descended onto enlisted mess halls and officers' messes. No thought was at that moment given to Vietnam or Russian subs. No one even thought of getting home. All of us on staff were posing possible conspiracy venues—"Johnson with his Texas connection" was first dibs in front of KGB, North Vietnamese, North Korea, Military-Industrial Complex (because Kennedy was planning to pull out of Vietnam). All humbug, of course. A future media acquaintance, lke Pappas, (RIP) whom I always remembered from his Vietnam posts for CBS, was pushed out of the way by Jack Ruby "popping" former Marine shooter, Lee Harvey Oswald. The names spring to fingers as if it were yesterday, or last Thursday. Will we ever know for sure? For sure, however, is that our path into Vietnam was secure, if only as a cover for Johnson's putative war on poverty, "The Great Society." Or did I get that backward. Great Society covering for Vietnam.

We got back to San Diego a few days before Thanksgiving 1963. The duty staff bachelor, I got stuck with duty. A whole bird to myself and the messmen. That next year we operated exclusively in San Diego waters getting ready for a January '65 Flotilla deployment. Meanwhile, the Vietnam Conflict—then so called—"escalated" precipitously. I had never heard that word.

Then the Tonkin Gulf incident. As I sat in the "Admiral's Barge," the boss's personal small craft (Navy Captains have "gigs"; barges are black, gigs grey), the brass would chat disgustedly about the White House and Pentagon needing civilian eyes on the scene. Huh? August 2, 1964, some North Vietnamese torpedo boats got into it with SEVENTH FLEET ships, "The Maddox Incident." Wikipedia covers this in sufficient detail to avoid here. Suffice it to say, Congress gave a resolution that opened the way

to "escalation"—the automatic staircase with no early "off button."
It was later confirmed the incident was way overplayed, and way
beyond the scope of this writing except to illustrate the impact of
high ranking opinions influencing the thinking of a Navy Lieutenant
(Junior Grade), LT(j.g.). Assuredly, I wasn't alone; any junior officer
not thoroughly behind gearing up for a contest was considered a
"short timer" and my class ('61) was still short on active duty by
over two years—still, enough to lose some early classmates who
went Navy Air.

We departed San Diego Naval Station embarked in USS
CANBERRA (CAG 2) the first week in January 1965, and we had
no sooner past "1 S.D.," the first sea buoy, when a message came in
from Commander in Chief Pacific Fleet to be ready to present a
patrol plan for Vietnam—which turned out to be "Market Time"—
to COMPACFLT a day after arrival. Turn and burn time—heads
down, butts up! Careers were resting on the forthcoming briefing
performance. I am delighted to write that the plan was well received,
some bumps, but generally well received. Comprehensive, cogent,
and coherent—daring redundancy. The plan outlined what became
known as Operation MARKET TIME, which over time grew
into an ocean surveillance effort—or at the least South China Sea
regional effort. It described destroyers, Swiftboats—the boss and I
visited the first in-country Swiftboat in Danang—indigenous junk
force squadrons with naval advisors, massive coastal support bases
extending the length of South Vietnam, and land based patrol aircraft.
The staff had arranged a P2 flight down the coastline to familiarize
the admiral with, essentially, the magnitude of the patrol area and
littoral—that early reference to beachfront property—hideouts. We
stopped at various air facilities and visited with the local U.S. Navy
advisory staffs to hear it "from the horse's mouth"—from Vung Tau

to Danang. The entire trip lasted two days. The MARKET TIME adventure had started from a ripple that reached all the way back to Washington's Bureau of Naval Personnel responsible for identifying and training advisors and crews for Swiftboat squadrons, and the initial buildup of a Riverine Force with which growing SEAL Teams would operate. Imagine this: sleepy San Diego, a quiet Navy homeport and training command infrastructure with shipyards and barely a skyline, got a central nerve shock around summer 1965 when I started UDT Replacement Training—next chapter. Boats, people, staff expansion, Marines, too, bulking up in Camp Pendleton—more ships: mindful of the current re-balance policy to Asia. I think one could establish 1965 as a renaissance year for San Diego. Aforementioned personnel growth, ships and aircraft, all impacting an unprepared civil-military population. In Coronado, the perky little Mexican Village—nickname "MexPac" (for reasons left obscure) and owned by a former Canadian hockey player—until then a cozy bar with a sing-along piano and cheap beer, resilient/ forgiving police force, and a couple of aircraft squadrons— "Fighter Town" at Miramar was a couple years off; with the best romaine salad in California—but hardly prepared to seat hundred of officers and enlisted "volunteers"—presented an enormous challenge to city fathers (and mothers) from Tia Juana to Del Mar. And what restaurant opportunities on both sides of the Bay!

My first San Diego encounter was 1955. When I got to Naval Training Command as a Naval Enlisted Striker, August 1955, downtown San Diego had its near-beer "Sailor Section," seedy bars, Army-Navy outlets, barber shops, laundries, and short-time, one-lightbulb rooms. I was out for two-week reserve boot camp—okay, respect, "Reserve Boot Camp." We got a Saturday noon time liberty to be back by midnight. We had a burger (no McDonald's), caught two John Wayne WW II movies, Chinese dinner, and were back by 2300 (11PM). My next San Diego "forever visit" was summer 1961. The sociological culture shock to San Diego and environs was that summer.

My time on COMCRUDESFOT SEVEN staff was nearing an end. The ships were more or less rotating around Danang, subbing for Monkey Mountain air search radar, and wondering when we'd get to shoot something. It was a boring time, except for some of the people we got to meet. As an Aide, I was responsible to the Admiral for protocol arrangements. Beyond delivering brownies to General Karch in Danang, I was responsible for flag menus. On one Danang anchorage occasion we hosted Lieutenant General Nguyen Van Thieu and his immediate staff to lunch. Simple fare—shrimp curry with several "side boy" condiments (shredded coconut, flecked bacons bits, onions, raisins, olives, celery, nuts, chopped hardboiled eggs). Conversation centered on flag reassurances to Thieu that we were there to help.

Since my temporary duty with CISM alerted me to underwater demolition and combat swimming—and I had become familiar with a lot of team people—noteworthy of whom was LCDR Bill Robinson, Naval Academy Class of '53, at the time Commanding Officer of UDT-12; he stood outside the recompression chamber as I took the pressure test. I had met him on a flight to Clark Air Base, Philippines, following my Barcelona competition. We had a rambunctious "arrival party" at the Clark O-Club where we were welcomed by a bevy of Flying Tiger hostesses, with whom I later linked up with in New York City. Robinson became an aide to the joint Commander of the Pacific Command. He and I later crossed paths in Newport, where he was in War College and I at Department Head School. From then on to Coronado and later—Bill got into real estate, and was surprisingly murdered while examining a tract of land, never solved. Robinson was on the other side of the SEAL commissioning effort. He felt Underwater Demolition Teams, with training, could be expanded to cover announced SEAL Team missions. Well, sometimes, when you're trying to make a statement and influence, you need some new "optics." It was clear to the office of Chief of Naval Operations (CNO) that UDTs had a repository of truncated land warfare capabilities. But the times, 1960–61, called for reemphasis. It was recognized that the UDTs were indispensable to the Amphibious Navy for beach reconnaissance and obstacle destruction prior to Marine landings. Emphasis on fully developing capabilities associated with maritime operations in and around riverine environments was evident it couldn't simply be tacked onto the list of UDT explosive support. Much discussion was bandied about in Washington. To summarize:

In March 1961, a branch of the Operations and Plans Directorate sent a SECRET memo to CNO: "1. *Problem.* How can the Navy improve its contribution to the U.S. guerrilla/counterguerrilla warfare capability?" It went laboriously into restricted waters capability, doctrinal guidance, personnel training, development and support of equipment, landing of troops, assault landings, reconnaissance, surveillance and patrolling, fire support, transport of supply, evacuation, communications, limited air support operations, and more. Subject to CNO approval, appropriate directives would be coordinated with OPNAV directories. It was approved.

Then, on May 13, 1961 (a month before my USNA graduation), another memo was sent CNO describing requirements to set up codes within OPNAV to address the items above, suggested personnel strength, and stressing the fleet UDTs were already chockablock with amphibious tasking—and speaks openly about special operations teams—and goes into more specialized recognition of what teams would clearly require. All of this was admittedly beyond Robinson's supposition fleet UDTs could assume the greater tasks. CNO approved the May memo and thus the programmatic wheels were set in motion albeit a good deal of IBM ink had already dried!

A month later, CNO informed the fleets of "Proposed Concept for Special Operations Teams (SEAL Units)"—June 5, 1961. SEAL Teams ONE and TWO were commissioned on January 1, 1962. Teams just completed celebrating a fiftieth anniversary in 2012. I was fortunate enough to be a joint author on a Naval Special Warfare/US NAVY SEAL Teams photo-anthology.

All this took place before my duty in Naval Special Warfare, so to continue . . . I was detached from CANBERRA late June with orders to report in July for UDT Replacement Training, which became Class 36. And so, onto my next "Navy Phase."

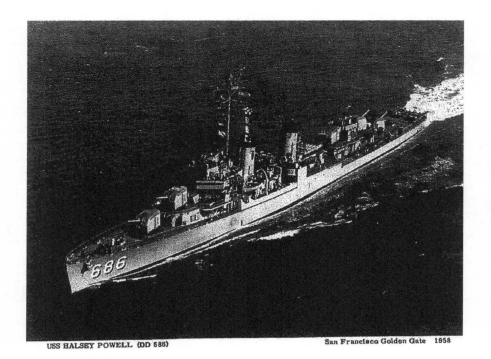

USS HALSEY POWELL (DD 686)   San Francisco Golden Gate   1958

http://www.navsource.orgfarchives/05/0568609.jpg   3/4/2015

Amphibious cross-country race, CISM Penthalon,
Karlskrona, Sweden 1963.

1964, CDR Ransom Arther (glasses), USN (MC), founder
of U.S. Masters Swimming, at a local San Diego meet.

CHAPTER 4

FIRST NAVAL SPECIAL
WARFARE ASSIGNMENTS

D eparted Commander Cruiser-Destroyer Flotilla SEVEN mid-
May 1965 after two years assignment. An interesting aspect of
the assignment was learning the inner workings of senior officer
staffs. I was an extremely junior officer, a Lieutenant Junior Grade
with just under four years' service. As interesting as inventing dinner
menus might prove for the new chef, there was a collateral aspect
to being an aide that took attention and some level of operational
diligence. During the Western Pacific deployment, I was assigned
by the admiral as staff Intelligence Officer. Briefly, this required me
to delve into the daily classified message traffic as well as purveying
published intelligence essays on the Vietnamese, the fractions, some
history, and order of battle—at least that arm that might affect the
ships assigned to the Flotilla's Destroyer Squadrons. I was required
to deliver an intel summary at the morning's message meeting, and
during daytime's sporadic reports came in. It was challenging and

basically dull, the challenge was to keep a modicum of interest in the material and still keep the immediate staff menu tasty.

But I was off—first, to Danang to hitch a C-130 Marine flight to Cubi, Point, from which I had to make it to Clark Air Base for the home leg. All pretty routing—check in to the Pax Terminal with orders and wait. It all worked flawless albeit time consuming. I was on leave for a month before the Underwater Demolition Team Replacement Training (UDTRA) class convened—some time to get into what I suspected was required conditioning. A little running, some long remembered swim workouts, pull-ups, chins, sit-up—nothing requiring particularly hard breathing. What a shock I was in for.

In those days, until 1970, UDTRA was conducted at Coronado, California, and Little Creek, Virginia. Was in the Coronado class. Officers underwent two weeks pre-training, to get them in shape to lead the enlisted students (trainees). My first day in ranks in green fatigues and boondockers boots was July 12, 1965, the day after my twenty-eighth birthday. First evolution—50-yard wind sprints, lots of them. I was shocked into disbelief: (1) that I was in such unsuspecting shape; (2) that the initial introduction was so "dynamic"—no auditorium advance briefing or "Welcome aboard, Gentlemen." The "into" was strictly kinetic. I felt like falling down in place. Hyperventilating like a cornered pig eyeing the castration blade! I wasn't alone I felt sure, but my eyesight was so truncated with exhaustion I was into tunnel vision, anybody not directly in front of me was unseen. Fortunately, the fainting wave subsided, and we shuffled off to Turner Field, so named after the World War II Pacific Theater amphibious commander, Vice Admiral Kelly Turner, for the introduction into UDTRA calisthenics—Physical Training, hereafter referred to as simply PT. One officer, out of approximately twenty, quit on the spot for inability to perform horizontal flutter kicks—the flutter kick with swim fins is the primary in-water source of propulsion for frogmen (and SCUBA divers everywhere). Also, I might add, that in the "old days" guys often volunteered for UDT to get orders off a particular ship. No deal today when SEAL Team volunteers are initially screened through Boot Camp—and about which more later.

Our initial officers' "welcome aboard" ended at lunch break, 1200-1300. The first afternoon was spent with an orientation introduction to the "Inflatable Boat, Small (IBS)," which we were promised would become second nature for boat crews. Thus ended our first relatively benign Monday. Let the games begin.

UDTRA in 1965—until military construction provided new buildings on the beach side of the base—was sited bayside, right on the water, with a boat ramp. We would soon learn that most evolutions in San Diego Bay would start from that ramp. Class had breakfast available in the crew's mess hall at 0530; muster at UDTRA was 0630 for an hour PT. Next, a slow "airborne shuffle" to the beach for a deep sand formation run, euphemistically referred to as a conditioning hike—four miles with an ocean plunge concluding; lunch in wet greens. Afternoon, tote the seven-man-crew IBS to the beach for three hours of surf passage. Fight the surf, dump boat, right boat, and ride the waves to shore trying not to broach—with initial rare success. That was Tuesday and Wednesday; Thursday was intro to the UDT obstacle course (O-Course). It's constructed with physical challenge in mind: parallel bars, high wall (10), balance beam steps phasing into a horizontal ladder, a three-story climbing platform with a forty-yard "slid for life" back down, several serial body scrunchers, a two-story high rope ladder (up one side, down the other), a two-foot-high barbed wire low crawl (to ensure you got sand on your greens), and a final vault obstacle, after which your time was recorded every Thursday; and you need constantly improving times throughout training. So, some gaming the O-Course came to mind; for example, speed up your end of course obstacles, as if instructors never ran the course. Any sign of sandbagging was fraught with risk. If a trainee didn't appear to be trying, he could find himself running it again.

All hands finished, time for a loosen up jog down the State Beach to check on the ice plants.

Friday was pool day with orientation on swim masks and fins, how to clear ears underwater, strokes, breathing techniques, life vest familiarization, and a one-mile pool swim around a buoy course—underwater recovery strokes, no over water reaching. We would spend more pool time the second week before we went into the bay. It was a breath-taking first week. The daily routine ended at 1600 every day. We would shuffle back to quarters to clean off uniforms and prep for the following day. Uniforms had to be starched pressed, boondockers spit shined (coke bottle best)—didn't matter if the boot was damp; it would be wet enough the next day! I would slink in, pick up a couple of Black Label beers from a BOQ vending machine, sit down in the community shower hot water, rinse out sand and beach scud, wring out uniforms, and hang to dry. Dinner at the O-Club at six, then take the damp uniforms out to a Coronado laundry for pressing. Back in the room, spit shine boots. Lights out at 2000 for a 0500 reveille. Sleep without dreams! The ship's wardroom seemed far away . . .

A note on blisters—deadly dangerous to one's future with frogmen. We were advised by some old-timers to buy white nylon socks and nylon skivvy shorts to avoid debilitating blisters from runs and sand. Feet are important as is the crouch area. Chapped thighs affected runs, blisters were out of action qualifiers. Infection was cause for dismissal; this was before the "phase" system of rolling back students. A note, daring to fast forward to 1989, as I was in process of relieving Rear Admiral Chuck Le Moyne at the Naval Special Warfare Command, he advised me of having introduced a "rollback" process whereby a qualified trainee could be rolled back into another class for reasons of physical disability, accident, or "case basis." In our day, a "drop" was final; you started the class all over again, including Hell Week. I made it a practice to interview graduating BUD/S officers the day of graduation. One officer had been turned back three times and spent eighteen months in training. I suspected he really wanted the program.

The enlisted students reported in the last week of July 1965, about sixty of them. No mercy either. We repeated all the familiarization drills we did in the officer two-week orientation with runs, PT, IBS surf passage—with longer paddles—and ocean surface swims up to two miles along Coronado Beach. Academically, we got into beach reconnaissance techniques to verify the beach depths and slope to the beach; UDT was responsible from the 21-foot depth to the beach high water line (high tide limit). Recordings were saved on plastic slates, which also noted the location of any other natural or man-made obstacles. One evolution worthy of recording was rock portage with IBS. The perfect topography for this are the surf rocks piled up in front of the majestic lady, Coronado's Del Coronado Hotel. These behemoths rise some twenty feet above the ground and are cause for massive crashing waves. Prospective frogmen trainees then and now practice on them—straight in, no looking for side shots. Landings are rehearsed in daylight; each boat crew gets a half-dozen times. Then the training moves to nighttime, much trickier. At all the trials a civilian hotel crowd gathers to gawk at the "commandos" from and acoustically respectful distance.

We did not lose any officers in the run-up to Hell Week; some enlisted sailors opted out back to the fleet. Hell Week, the grueling, six-night-no-sleep evolution of drills and exercises designed to eliminate uncommitted volunteers. In 1965, Hell Week started at 1700 Sunday and secured the following Saturday after morning PT. Our initiation began on time ... with the class butt-ass naked sitting on Marston Matting getting hosed down for an hour singing class songs. Sun still high in early August, we trundle enthusiastically over to Turner Field for a PT session before dinner, after which we went to the beach to jog and play surf follies, lying down in the shallow breakers—more singing. Five days of seemingly limitless evolutions; you never know when an evolution was over. One particularly psychological evolution was thought up by Navy Cross winner Barry Enoch (RIP). He would have us tie our kapok life preservers into a fifty yard line which then with IBS paddles we would march off the bayside pier into the water, line up, and sing songs for an hour. Out of the water, we hung our wet gear on our racks—thinking we were in for some sleep (this was Wednesday). All comfy, warm, dreamless sleep came inside a minute *boom!* An M80 firecracker, after fifteen minutes, harshly reminded us of reality. Greens and kapoks are still sopping wet and by now cold. Suit up, grab your paddle, form up, right face, move down the pier—splash, splash every man ... more singing. Same drill—back to barracks (right there), undress, dry off, dry skivvies, dark sleep, twenty minutes into deep soma—*kaboom!* Rise and shine—hoo yah! Outside, rig up, pick up paddle. March to the end of the pier. In my mind I was convinced if I had to go into that water one more time that was it. "Class halt, about face, secure and muster up on Turner Field!"

I'll never know, but I reassure myself that if the guy in front of me went, I was tied to him.

I need to mention the "Mud Flats," a muddy tidal pool south of the Del Coronado Hotel, close to Imperial Beach, today gone, host to a late sixties upscale housing development called the Coronado Cays. (I had a house there in 1982.) We visited the Mud Flats on the Thursday of Hell Week—all day. It's a five-mile IBS paddle from the PHIBASE. Lunch is served in the water—muddy water I should add (for veracity). We were covered with mud, playing games and flopping around in the mud. (It was warm.) The paddle home took over an hour. Thursday night was a "scavenger hunt" from the base to the North Island fence. Along the course route I would sing show tunes to the boat crew. "I like New York in June, how about you?" "A Foggy Day in London Town . . ." etc. It was a break from the "ring dang do" of class conditioning hike. We secured at 0300 for a 0400 wake up call.

Friday, pool races. Friday night, a night paddle to Imperial Beach. As we chugged down the Bay, my boat was leading, a blinking light from the "Point Golf" marker ordered us into the beach where we were informed we were lead boat for Hell Week, and were pulled out of the night's evolution. There was no energy for emotion or ecstasy, just quiet conversation with the leading instructor, and hour's paddle to the base to stow the IBS and hit the quarters. I got to bed at 0300 and woke up at 0700. I jogged down to Turner where the final Hell Week PT drill was; the rest of the class was then secured. I was dried and dressed. Training Hell Week's today close down Friday morning. It was determined that after Wednesday, those still there would finish; and the extra night demanded an extra week's recovery. (I have heard it takes six months to fully recover.) At that time I was dating a woman in La

Jolla, so I drove out there, ate a skimpy breakfast, and went to bed to sleep six hours. The rest of the weekend was fuzzy. No running the following two weeks, only stretching exercises, no O-Course, no long swims—just recoup before moving onto phase II, diving. The weekend after Hell Week we had a post-HW beach barbecue. Nothing overboard—burgers and potato salad and a couple of keg beers. We were still going to bed at eight o'clock!

Two final phases: diving and San Clemente. Diving taught us compressed air (open circuit) scuba and closed circuit pure oxygen (no bubbles) diving. Students had to pass the pool open circuit course, which included a harassment swim wherein instructors would attempt to disorient the diver. You have to pass to progress. Class 36 passed. We moved to bat underwater compass swims of up to a mile, day and night. The oxygen course was more technical in that setting up the diving rig is strict—then and now. All passed.

Last phase was three weeks at the compound at San Clemente Island, 83 miles west of San Diego. It was, in 1965, a pure replica of a lean to shanty town—plywood floors, slats for windows, crickety metal racks, two high WW II holdover hand-me- downs. Shaving and showers were done with cold water. But all showers were far was washing the salt out of uniforms. Reveille was 0600 every morning regardless of how late the night op lasted. Briefings were done by the trainees; if the Lane Grader wasn't satisfied with the brief, stop the show—restart the briefing on "Student Time." If the faulty briefing went down at 1900 and a "restart" command was given, turn the clocks back to "1900." Fortunately, we suffered only a couple of these.

The long of it, at the island, was to learn demolitions and small arms. There were night problems for patrol exercises—much more intense nowadays. Our focus was loading submerged obstacles, called "scullys." We learned how to fabricate "double waterproof firing assemblies," an arrangement of two fuses and detonators wired into Detcord and activated by a length of time fuse calculated to explore at a pre-programmed time—long enough to get the swimmers to clear the area. The first two days were spent free diving with 20-pound sacks of C3. The scully was positioned about the 15-foot depth; hyperventilate, dive down, and with one or two repeat dives tie in the demo to the obstacle. When done an instructor would paddle board out, dive down, and try to rip your placement off the obstacle. My swim buddy was a two-pack-a-day smoker. By the first day's lunch break, we hadn't loaded our first scully. We still had the four to go. We finally accomplished the task, but to that point in the entire course, loading obstacles was the hardest thing I had encountered. San Clemente also afforded the long swim opportunity—six mile fin swim off the island. The sea lions were everywhere, curious about the new intruders. Happily, no sharks. Roosevelt and I were first in for the hot coffee. The next day was Thanksgiving and, yes the instructors had turkeys and the trimmings for us. God bless 'em. We got the afternoon off then mustered for the night problem.

I recall it rained just about every day. And no wearing wet suit tops! It rained both days of obstacle loading. No problem; the hardest was the rain at night. Paddling into the beach, patrolling around the island—all in a late November rain. We had a final battle problem, which included loading out ten sculleys planted by the staff from a PHIBASE LCU. Our job was to swim in, locate the obstacles, and next day blow 'em. Only the second day had the sun shown; the weather, while cool, was magnificent. We got 100 percent clearance of the field with no misfires. Our way was clear for a Friday, December 3, 1965 graduation, which was held in the

Amphibious School Auditorium to a small audience. (Graduations today are big events at the Naval Special Warfare Center.) The whole course lasted four-and-a half months, from July 12 to December 3. Thirty of us closed out Class 36 (ten officers, twenty enlisted). Today's course has a basic course of three, seven-week phases followed by six months advanced SEAL tactics. In 1965, classes had to fall in line for Army Jump School. Specialized courses were still followed depending on need. I went to Jump School at F. Benning, Georgia, February 1966. The actual jumps were into neighboring Alabama. I remember my first one, at the risk of getting ahead of myself. The plane overran the drop zone just as I was getting to the door. A big ham fist caught my harness and a voice barked out, "Hold on, Captain (my Navy 'railroad tracks' Lieutenant are Captains in other services) we're taking it around!" So I sat down by the door and looked out at the Alabama farmlands. Command came, "Stand up, hook up. Go! Last to land but a perfect, lonely solo static-line, first jump. On the Team with Army Jump Wings.

What'd I learn? Endurance, which I will expand on in my UDTRA chapter.

CHAPTER 5

POST SCRIPT: TRAINING FOR UNDERWATER DEMOLITION (UDT/SEAL)

A
t the risk of redundancy, let me add a postscript to my proceeding chapter about Underwater Demolition Replacement Training (UDTRA). There are no words to share the exhaustion, stress, or view of a near horizon to completion of a UDT-SEAL trainee. "Once a trainee, always a trainee" became a stigma shared by one in all in training. "The only easy day was yesterday" became the adopted litany—offered by a succeeding class—that fairly accurately established the culture of UDTRA Training (today called Basic Underwater Demolition/SEAL Training or "BUD/S") as a mindset. Once accepted, the challenge becomes somewhat more rational.

In my 1965 day, officers were required to complete two weeks "private" indoctrination to get them in shape and familiar with the UDTRA discipline and routine. Our first line up was Monday morning, July 12, a day after my twenty-eighth birthday . . . and I had just pinned on "Lieutenant" bars. The class senior officer was a lieutenant too.

I wrote about training extensively in a photo-anthology I co-authored in 2012. This time I think I will emphasize how it affected me on a personal level. Writing on "a corporate level," backed with photographs and captions, is a bit more sterile than wiping the sweat from your own brow. Whew! But I hadn't discovered real "whew" yet. As a former age-group swimmer and high school three sport participant, I had learned how to pant and pace. UDTRA, and today's title, "Basic Underwater Demolition/SEAL (BUD/)," disabused all of us the possibility of pacing anything. UDTRA and BUD/S are anything but little league, Pop Warner, U.S. swimming, varsity sports workouts. So, as an experienced athlete, most lately (then) the 1963 All Navy Pentathlon Champion and U.S. representative to CISM Swimming Championships. And I had kept up training all through 1964 and during five months of the Flotilla deployment—kept my Halsey Powell Christmas Island routine active. Did get a little slack during leave, but that would get a knot jerked into it immediately. Day one, UDTRA Class 36, fall in . . . for a few wind sprinters jus' to get everyone's attention. I was breathing so hard I felt I was going to pass out. These were cheap little 50-yard lopes at the edge of the Bay. (UDTRA then was housed on the Bay side of the Naval Amphibious Base.) But we weren't in shorts and sneakers; we were in full utility greens and boondockers. I actually felt like fainting! One of those "life passing before your eyes" moments. Surprise, I stuck in. Recouped, our two-dozen officers then caught their breaths and headed to Kelly Turner Field—named for the WW II Amphibious commander. An hour of Physical Training (PT).

We were introduced to UDT pushups—the correct performance thereof; chin-ups; flutter kicks (on your back, hands crossed under your lower back, legs straight, toes pointed . . . "Ready, begin . . . down one, down two, down three . . . down fifty . . . (puff, puff); now some stretching drills, which angels your joints didn't recognize. Flutter kicks, one officer could not even do one; he quits that morning. By now we were warmed up—San Diego summer, July 12. Time to introduce the Silver Strand, six miles from North Island Naval Air Station to the State Beach south abutting Imperial Breach. And the topographic highlight of this stretch of littoral is sandunes—soft-sanpunes and dunes—up and down, up and down, up and down for miles. Oh, "Class, hit the surf!" The system shock from Pacific Ocean cold water is hard to describe. Winter, spring, summer, fall . . . it's always cold. But now fully soaked, let's roll in the hot, dry sand. Don't worry, class, we'll hit the surf once before returning to the main base for a wet lunch. Let's go get our rubber boats and learn about paddling and surf passage. Two hours, 1400-1600. First day.

After being secured (Navy term meaning quit), we made our way back to the Bachelor Officer Quarters (BAQ). There was a community shower; I cracked two Black Label beers and sat under the hot water rinsing sand out of my greens and boondockers, which had to be spit shined by the next morning (use a Coke bottle). Dinner in the O-Club, back to the room to prep clothes for the second day of Hell. Breakfast 0530, PT muster 0630—let the day begin! Every day got increasingly more aggressive in terms of run and swim distance. No ocean swimming yet, only pool and bay; always interlaced with PT and the new monster, the obstacle course ("O" Course). It was run every Thursday throughout training, followed by soft sand runs. Two weeks of this officers-only indoctrination. Our class had good performers in the water and overall. After the first few days the weak people dropped on request ("DOR" henceforth). By the end of two weeks we had our class officers; none dropped later, all graduated.

Let's get some things understood. UDT—and later, SEAL—training is not about athletics. Sure, physical stamina and strength are cornerstones for "frogmen"; ya gotta have endurance and ya gotta be able to shoulder (literally) the proverbial load—lots a weight on your back and, in training, rubber boats. The commands are referred to as "teams," yes, but it is the coordinated working relationships among teammates and joint groups that matters in combat, not average scores, or midcourt shots, or Olympic qualifying times for runs or swims. I thought it unhelpful to belabor this, but in fact, it is imperative that understanding of Naval Special Warfare basic and advanced training that standards have been developed since 1943 and earlier should a historical itch entice a reader.

Let me explain, endurance is necessary for long patrols and various maritime operations in boats or swimming. Since the early eighties, shipboard assaults have been developed, whereby SEALS climb up scaling ladders to board suspected ships—this with small arms, radios, flak jackets, sundry tools for explosive breeching techniques, and protective headgear. On occasion, diving rigs are hefted up too. Being able to do this requires strength—rope climbing strength; for swimming, fin kicking; for overland endurance, running. The underlying philosophy of UDTRA (now BUD/S) is going beyond burn, past ostensible muscular failure.

BUD/S, which I now transition to, is not a team "sport" per se. The physical training that culminates with five days of uninterrupted drills referred to as "Hell Week, is fashioned to take a man, not yet woman, down to survival body weight yet ensures healthy stamina to perform on distance runs and extended surface swims. And don't forget the O-Course, in which each week a trainee must improve his time. One can invent a pace methodology to, say, sandbag the first few obstacles, speeding up the time from the last obstacle week to week. Okay, if it's a believable performance, but it suspected of malingering, the Pacific Ocean awaits after which dunking the contestant gets to run the course again. Don't be late, dear . . . the class will wait cheering the malingerer on to success! The nitty-gritty of negotiating the lower sand-crawling obstacles in wet greens is a torture all on its own.

Two weeks officers-only went fast. On August 1 thirty enlisted sailors reported in. Boat crew assignment were made, and a new societal fabric was established. The "Os" by now knew the deal, as it were; it takes a while to get into the culture of BUD/S. First to be learned was the chant driven elocution, "hoo yah," which was a required response to every situation—from instructor admonishment to encouraging classmate's performances, like urging a laggard O-Course performance. The daily training day was 0600. Normally, first event was P.T. on Turner Field followed by a distance jog on the Strand up and down the dunes. Oh, for that occasional step on a patch of ice plant, otherwise each step in the soft sand drove your hips further into your chest! There is a technique to soft sand running, point your toes at the point of attack into the sand. This shapes the foot purchase by creating a divot from which your foot can push off toward the direction you're going. Takes getting used to. Of course you are expected to keep in step with the song you're chanting. August is warm in San Diego, so the welcome reprieve to "hit the surf" was met with thunderous "hoo yahs."

Much time in basic is spent during surf passage. What good is a Frogman who can't negotiate the ocean waves? We passed with fins and IBS, the principal drill was to paddle out beyond the zone, dump the boat over, right it, and head for shore. Takes a while to get the hand of it. Tardy or inept crews got to put the boat down and get into push-up position with feet up on the gunnels—then begin to "push away" the State of California. Lotsa fun. "Hoo yah, boat crew five!" And to mention class punishment. Sloppy maneuvers might result in a two-mile jaunt with boat on heads up and over the dunes—all hands praying for ice plant patches. Closer to nature than ever imagined.

Another challenging and scary event is negotiating huge rocks fronting the breakwater in front of the Hotel Del Coronado, a surprising sprite lady for a nineteenth century hotel. The rocks are approached from sea by our rubber boats, seven trainees in each boat crew. The "rock pile" is some twenty feet above the low water line, black, jagged, and crookedly piled with UDT-SEAL trainees in mind. Our day uniform was greens, sand boots (boondockers), kapok life jackets, and floppy hats fastened to your shirt. (Today, helmets are worn—pussies!) Naturally, no one or no team has any idea how to get the boat over the rock pile, so the individual episodes are accomplished with a few hundred push-ups. We learn how to do it in daylight; night passage comes later when we were tougher and more confident. Confidence comes with time, but it's still a challenging evolution. Like every training event, it's wet, cold, dark, and long.

"Hell Week" occurs on the fifth week of BUD/S; starts with compound breakout Sunday evening and secures Friday morning around 1000. In 1965 FINEX was Saturday morning after P.T. It was changed because it was determined the extra twenty-four hours added a week to recuperate. And by Thursday drops are rare; most come the first two days. Class 36 started at 1700 Sunday with the class stripped naked(!) on Marston Matting (metal sheets for advance runways), huddled down to be hosed for an hour whilst singing songs the class wrote. ("I don't know but I've been told . . .") Following the drenching, orders came out of the loud speaker to get dressed in five minutes for Hell Week introductory P.T. It's now six-thirty; an hour later, repare to the mess hall for evening meal. It's still sunny outside, early August. Following the rushed meal, we mustered back at our "Inflatable Boat, Small (IBS)"—these are carried everywhere during Hell Week—for a seven-mile paddle in San Diego Bay. I've lost all recollection to time; it's probably 11:30 PM (2330). Back to the bayside headquarters to prep for a euphemistically-termed "night problem." Hoisting the boats on our heads, we traversed the Amphibious Base and headed to the Strand Beach for night surf passage. Out beyond the surf zone to ride the waves.

Back to barracks for one hour nap…and that was it. Period. M80 firecracker in a metal trash can—hard to accept as part of a dream. Out to the grinder for 0500 P.T. Then breakfast and the day repeats. Nobody dropped so far and it's Monday, or whatever; I've even lost count of the days typing this. Pool drills—long Hell Week swims without fins in the base pool. Underwater recovery strokes, no overhead strokes, basically side stroke with scissor kick. At least the water was warm. I remember one swim; all with face mask you could see people around you. If you were fast you could pass the slower swimmers. I noticed a couple of guys cheating on turns—turning inside the buoy markets. Indignant, I swam to the pool's edge, emerged, and reminded the staff it was their duty to ensure compliance, etc., etc. I wasn't at all sure if that would sit well, but I was a lieutenant and kids were cheating under the instructors' noses.

Other drills were structured to piss us off, like cutting short a meal. These were sacrosanct periods . . . well, perfect to get into a trainee's head. One night, at the midnight hour, this one instructor—great guy, Navy Cross SEAL—rigged the class in kapoks and paddles and tied us all to a line. We marched off the end of the boat dock into the Bay for choir practice—one hour floating with paddles singing class songs. "Recover"—back to barracks wet and ready to sleep. Wet greens hung in our quarters when *boom!* M80 in the shit can. This was after ten minutes of nodding off. Regroup outside, same rope line. Marched off the pier—more songs. One hour. "Recover!" By now we were getting into "brrr" time. Hit the rack, sawin' serious zzzzz's. *Boom!* Ditto the routine. Back into now cold soggy greens and kapoks, hut-two-three-four. (If I have to jump into that Bay one more time I'm outta here.) "Class halt! About face, forward march!" to Turner Field. Whew! P.T. was a snap compared to that chilly water!

Hell Week is hallmarked with funny routines designated to test adaptability under stress, mental and physical. Log P.T. is a piece of cake, it's not heavy unless you have to lift it alone. The major challenge is cold water. I was fortunate to have the winning boat crew. Thursday night we had a scavenger treasure hunt night problem—dare I note an all-night treasure hunt, with IBS on heads throughout, all over the PHIBASE. On the North Coronado beach, running as we could, I would keep pace with the boat crew by singing show tunes along the route. "I like New York in June… A foggy day in London town…Oklahoma…etc." (I forget all the words today; fortunately, my reputation didn't suffer!)

Friday night was a Bay IBS transit race. From the PHIBASE down to the city dump where the Coronado Cays 1970 development is today. Our boat was in the lead and was signaled in to Point

GOLF, a marker in the Diego Bay. We were informed we had won the Hell Week boat competition, and were rewarded by being secured early. It was about 9:00 PM. After the rest of the class continued paddling south, we were told to paddle back to base and secure from Hell Week. It took us an hour to get back—tide? Wash off IBS, shower, etc. I hit the Sack around 0200 to awake at 0700. I jogged down to Turner Field to see the class finishing P.T. "It pays to be a winner," the adage pounded into our fragile brains throughout Hell Week. I was dating a woman in La Jolla at the time. I went there in a cloud, and collapsed for six hours. The day before I had experienced some humongous heel blisters. Luckily, they did not get infected. It took the class two weeks to recover, and lore has it that it really takes six months. Ho hum. The following two weeks we were not to jog. PT was gentle stretching exercises. The first Saturday after Hell Week we had a beer party on the beach. The class proctor was the only instructor. I should have introduced this luminary sooner. Second Class Petty Officer Vince Olivera, a full-blooded Apache, direct to us from the MGM back lot and one of the most competent people I have ever met. He would pace our runs with a Rum Crook cigar. He was admired and respected by all trainees. His private/personal advice was welcome.

Phase two was diving—open circuit and closed circuit scuba. Open circuit is compressed air; closed is pure oxygen rebreathers. Air scuba has bubbles, oxygen is without bubbles. Our dive instruction began in the pool and progressed to the San Diego Bay. Dives up to a mile were accomplished with open and closed scuba. A test of scuba training is the pool certification training, which includes a scuba harassment swim where instructors labor to interrupt a swim by inflicting attacks on your rig. Knock off your dive mask, interrupt the air flow; rip off a fin; turn off your regulator—big wicket to pass before moving on. Our class passed. (In fact, we only lost one guy when the boat ramp fell on his leg! He went through a later course.)

Following dive phase, the class delved into land patrolling—inland demolition raids, more aptly. These began in the Korean War as valid UDT missions. One week was devoted to "escape and evasion" as an accompanying drill to the inland demo portion. It was called the "Colorado River Week," wherein boat crews had five days to negotiate the Colorado River between Cooper and Hover dams with IBS rubber boats and roughly five days "C-Rats," travelling only by night and laying up during day to avoid detection, like Soviet scouts searching for us in some Third World enclave; actively portrayed by the duty instructors infused with several cases of beer. The drill was to evade "capture," which event was usually forecast at Moab whereupon half the rations were confiscated and the imprudent boat crew sent a-sea to finish the week on the river. All boats were intercepted, and crews underwent feigned interrogation—close to today's experience of water boarding.

The favorite C-Rats meal was the ham and beans. We occasionally lit a fire to warm the coffee; C-Rats went down cold. We would shove off at sunset and lay up an hour before sunrise, everyone exhausted. In some areas it was necessary to portage the rubber boat (with rations inside) for several yards because of low water for paddling. We would shift off coxswain duty. I recall lying down in the middle of the boat and be asleep before my head touched the rubber tube! And this was the second time I hallucinated. The first, Hell Week night paddling back to base when I was sure we went past Roman aqueducts. On the river, the mountains turned into dinosaurs, and I saw a nineteenth century couple standing in the water, watching us paddle by. Real as today. Everyone got along fine. We saw no rattlesnakes, coyotes, mountain lions, or bears, some harmless tarantulas and lizards and lots of birds. As fatiguing as the trip was, it was a welcome respite from daily PT, runs, O-Course, scuba dives with stingrays, and ball-breaking soft-sand runs in boondockers. The river week ended soon after when Vietnam captured the commands' attention—a regretful loss of a real bonding experience. Our bus stopped one time for a beer on the ride back to Coronado and a shower and shave.

Phase III: three rainy, dismal weeks at San Clemente Island, 83 miles off San Diego, for demolition and small arms training plus some UDTRA games and tricks. Each phase seemed to have its own unique culture. San Clemente was primarily about explosives; but land patrolling was also undertaken all over the island. Offshore IBS insertions, rock climbing, walking, walking, walking. And the most challenging event was first—loading inshore obstacles—free diving with Hagersacks (20-pound C4 explosive packs). My dive buddy was a smoker, case closed, we barely made to cutoff. And it rained every day except Thanksgiving! Every night problem was in the rain. No wet suit tops allowed. Tramping up and down the island and swooning in IBS boats offshore awaiting a blinking flashlight spark to order each boat in through the midnight surf. A major event was (remains) a six-mile surface swim with fins. My swim buddy, Ensign Ted Roosevelt IV, and I were first in for the coffee. Brrrr . . . two cups with sugar! It was a dismal three weeks, probably for the instructors as well. We passed, we survived, we hung in, and we went home—an eight hour LCM ride that could have passed for a carnival cruise. And we graduated with a minimum graduation ceremony in the Amphibious School auditorium. The senior visitor was Senator Smathers, Bruce's dad. (Bruce was in our winning Hell Week boat crew.) But we were beyond ceremonies and speeches. We were free. At some point in training you look at yourself as a trainee forever.

And fast forward to 2015. There is serious discussion about allowing women into combat jobs, including special operations, the argument being that if they are physically qualified, why shouldn't they be allowed to test out and serve in hazardous assignments? I'm ready to argue about it and opine that close quarters of men in SEAL team operations is totally dependent on the bonding teammates form during work-up and exercises. I don't see it working, even beyond the strength standards, it's the psychological dynamic between the sexes that would not add one iota to combat efficiency. Author George Gilder wrote a book in 1993 titled *Men and Marriage* (Pelican Publishing), which among other societal commentary examines the women in combat issues. Against it, he concludes with, briefly, "The consequence of this latest demand for equality would be nothing more or less than a move toward barbarism. (Page 136)" Britain Anne Moire coauthored a book about the same time called *Brain Sex*, which laboriously describes the biological differences between male and female brains that determine how each sex performs and act. Suffice it to say, much effort is given to attaching push-ups and chin-ups to operational requirements driving standards, perhaps neglecting the differences, with all due reverence to Rudyard Kipling's 1911 "The Female of the Species":

> "When the Himalayan peasant meets the he-bear in his pride, He shouts to scare the monster, who will often turn aside.

But the she-bear thus accosted rends the peasant tooth and nail. For the female of the species is more deadly than the male."

So how's the Marine Corps doing adapting women in the Infantry Officers' Corps? SEAL training is best summed up in our adage, "The only easy day was yesterday." Training is not to develop a highly conditioned athlete. It's for military conditioning to withstand stress, lack of sleep, food, fear, and uncertainty. Anything added to the curriculum that does not produce combat effectiveness doesn't belong. Some attributable unknown Army colonel once is said to have quipped, "SEALs are Olympic athletes with guns." Well, that's a flawed snapshot at best even with several Olympians who served, like butterfliers Mike Troy and Fred Schmidt. Troy served with UDT-11 in Vietnam in Operation *Jackstay (1966)*. The majority of SEALS and frogmen were high school athletes but not all were. Many of the officer candidates did play on college teams (I a Naval Academy swimmer), but not all did. The determinate of who survives BUD/S training makes the team roster.

I noted earlier that training changes over the years, but still maintains the first phase scrub orientation to determine who really wants to belong in the SEAL program. My class was four-and-a-half months, but we worked Saturday mornings too. Today's BUD/S course is three seven-week phases as before: selection, diving, small units tactics (demolition and small arm)—twenty-one weeks total. Next is SEAL Qualification Training (SQT) which is six months and covers among things exotic equipment, small arms, communications, land navigation, and parachuting (static line and freefall). Classes in the second half of the sixties got combat orientation fast, some without jump school, which I will highlight later.

What'd I learn in UDTRA? Perseverance. I'd been down the perseverance road twice before—South Kent and the Naval Academy. Although South Kent was decidedly less brutal than USNA, there is a mindset that gets people through challenging periods. "Plebe Year" at all service academies are pretty much cleansing/tempering rituals to determine who can endure stress and maintain academic equilibrium. Sports were essentially an informal "time out" for athletes. No upper class messes with Plebes during practice. And during the actual seasons, varsity sports teams enjoy training tables—different menu. Still, Plebe Year is an eleven-month ordeal to eliminate those with second thoughts about being at an academy. To this end, the year becomes a unique challenge that enlarges into an end in itself. Persevering becomes the order of the day. Of course, when the football team wins, Plebe get "carry on." Basically, relaxation at meals, no bracing up. Suck it up, it ends Monday morning. And an aside, there is no darker day than that day when the Christmas holiday ends and Midshipmen report back to the academy—the sun's been down since four o'clock (1600) and the noise of Plebes calling out evening meal reverberates throughout Bancroft Hall. Welcome back to the aptly named "dark ages." There is no day on any year's calendar more depressingly black than that first night back. I was to learn there are "black days" in the fleet as well. Persevere, hang in there. "The only easy day was yesterday!"

And Endurance, not the kind you experience during PT or a beach run; but the longer term kind that encompasses reveille, lunch, and the last evolution of a day, any day. It's more keeping faith with the "horizon goal," graduation and assignment to a team; to be counted as among the elite. It's the desire to achieve a challenging goal, to resist the easy way to a hot shower and the rack. It's sticking alongside classmates. It's not quitting. Kick me out, drop me on performance, but I'll never quit. Of course, every trainee enters the front door committed to success. Something changes along the way. An interesting tidbit: most BUD/S voluntary drops occur during the first two days of Hell Week—Sunday night, Monday night, Tuesday night—by Wednesday morning most remaining will finish. Which is not to say that training can be condensed into those three nights. Wednesday morning sunrise shines on the majority who'll succeed. Ha! "the sun also rises" on winners and losers!

Surf passage.

The rocks on the beach of the Dell Coronado Hotel.

CHAPTER 6

UNDERWATER DEMOLITION TEAM ELEVEN

UDTRA graduation, Friday, December 3, 1965, all classmates with orders in hand for assignments to operational UDTs. I cannot remember any Coronado graduates going to East Coast teams, all slated for UDT-11 and UDT-12. My first commanding officer was Lieutenant Commander Norman Olson a.k.a., "Stormin' Norman," a well-deserved cognomen. Direct, competent, and capable, Olson went on to command Naval Special Group two and the Little Creek Amphibious Base. He was, after retirement, the founder of the UDT-SEAL Museum in Ft. Pierce, Florida.

I reported into the team the Monday following graduation. Christmas leave period was on most minds at that point. Half the team was deployed under the Executive Officer (XO), Lieutenant John Callahan, who had been the commissioning commanding officer for SEAL Team TWO in Little Creek, Virginia (January 1, 1962). In those days Underwater Demolition Teams split overseas deployments between two half-teams: Team 11 for a year, Team 12 for a year, allowing for one-in-four six-month split deployments. This arrangement afforded the men a year and half for home port family time. It allowed time for schools, ample allocation of platoons for local fleet exercises, and out-of-area schools like Jump School (three weeks). The opportunity for training and schools was limited only by imagination and initiative ... as long as the recommendation made sense and funding available (not always). I recall later in SEAL Team ONE sending people for skiing and sailing lessons; locksmith, outboard engine maintenance, diesel engine repair, various communications and electronics school, Special Forces (Army) medic/corpsman school at Ft. Bragg, jumpmaster course, diving supervisor, Intel course at Fort Huachuca, Arizona, cold weather training in Alaska. All these academic accomplishment added a Navy Enlisted Classification Code (NEC) to a man's record, which helped with promotion to a higher paygrade. Thus the training schedule.

Another psychological aspect attached to the master training sked: ages of Frogmen. For the "Old Salts," a quarter-year or half-year go by lick idly split; for the younger men it's timeless. Younger guys needed more repetition to digest the training rationale, missions, safety regulations, behavior requirements; building character is a lifelong endeavor—maturing requires attention, dedication, and commitment. Goofing off had its immediate pleasure but often time incurs penalty. The Navy Frogman has legal guides the civilian counterpoint does not. The Uniform Code of Military Justice (UCMJ) is the legal bible of comportment. Immediately, before nudging lawyers, team regulations as derived from service and fleet instructions generally close the loop on personal activities in effect to guide the command in mission performance. Then individual safety rules and regulations and platoon operating mores guide all members in daily performance standards and expectations. In my experience, infractions are rare but too often in cause and effect and conclusions in our business are written in blood. In the Navy Air world, an expression is, "That's the break of Naval Air." In Naval Special Warfare, diving, demolitions, small arms, parachuting, and the unknowns of topography demand full attention. Here is where the master training plan must capture the attention of all, old and young.

I was to learn that UDT and SEAL enlisted, up until mid-2000s, served in Navy ratings or job descriptors like engineman, radioman, boilerman, in which the individual sailor competed with his fleet counterpart for promotion. Our guys normally performed well, but it was challenging to learn Special Operations and keep a fleet skill current. When platoons departed on cruise it presented an opportunity for people to integrate with shipboard sailors to polish off the bookwork with hands on experience, to the chagrin of Bureau of Naval Personnel (BUPES) rating monitors. Such was the World (capital "W") I was entering!

Not long on the team, I got a call from the "acting X.O.," because Callahan was deployed, to get with him about a San Diego request for a demolition display for the groundbreaking ceremony of the San Diego Stadium, future home of the San Diego Chargers football team and currently named Qualcomm Stadium. We discussed feasibility, ground rules for safety, and artistic attractiveness of the event. We sent for Navy Chief John Clancy, long-time frogman and leading chief in the Demolition Department. Clancy put some thought to what could be achieved using timed delay fusing arrangements. His suggestions were enthusiastically supported and we got to it. The plan: three demonstrations. First, an outline of the baseball diamond by explosions starting on the pitcher's mound, home base, around the bases, and back to home. Quarter pound TNT charges would be under blocks of colored patio powder used to color cement and time fused to follow each other around the diamond—six distinct "booms" football. Two shots, first a simple outline of the playing with succeeding shots from the 50-yard line, 25, goal line—three "booms." Finale, colored smoke flares attached to each of the goal posts, all fired simultaneously with simple det cord cutting the flare spoons, the smoke to carry down field with the incoming west wind. Baron Hilton pushed the plungers and it went down sweeter that warm toast! *Whew,* I said to myself, *live another day.* Chief Clancy and his team of demolitioners did a magnificent job. Sheriff's Department kept the field safe, and the shots weren't overly loud.

From the anxiety of that first assignment, I was locked into learning the culture of the team, which meant experiencing the expectations of the C.O. and the officers. Coming as I was from two years shipboard experience and two on a major staff, I was basically equipped with a sense of responsibility. Orders in the U.S. Navy are acknowledged with a curt "Aye, aye, Sir!" A response I learned Plebe Year. Frogmen might embellish the response with a tailing "Hoo yah!" But more worrisome to me was getting the officers junior to me to come in with weekly platoon training recommendations that reflected the needs of the forthcoming deployment—daily schedules that went beyond "PT and a run." It was an uphill challenge. Their chore was to sit with their chiefs and dope out what a given platoon might need in the way of formal NEC schooling—and getting quotas wasn't a cake walk; often it took months to get a class quota, a frustration learned early in my Halsey Powell assignment (and would continuously encounter my entire Navy career. It was "tail wagging the dog").

In February 1996, a detachment of us from both west coast teams went back to Fort Benning, Georgia, for basic static line parachute, A teams had added the jump requirement around 1962 and strove to meet a 100 percent fill. It was instructive learning the Army Airborne marching songs—or chants, if you will. The physical demands of Jump School were minimal for UDTRA grads. When compared the ten push-up penalties invoked on violators with the "100" required on our basic school. Running was a joke, consider it as never happening. I'm not complaining here. The Army's mission was to make safe, competent parachutists out of farm boys leaving the physical stress to their home battalions.

Jump School had three weeks, as I noted. Week one was ground school, learning to land from five-foot platforms using a parachute landing fall (PLF), which entailed five points of body contact with Mother Earth. After the first two days of jumping, hitting, and rolling I had headaches by 5:00 PM—definitely beer time. Week two was familiarization with the parachute, wearing harnesses, aircraft procedures. Stand up, check equipment, sound off, hook up. Then the airborne shuffle to the door and the leap into the Alabama air column—in February cold as hell. Week three, jump week; five static line jumps for the basic airborne wings, which were affixed to the student's tunic right on the drop zone—all the ceremony once could with for, lots of proud troopers. Some of those kids probably never landed in an airplane until they got to Saigon. My fourth jump eliminated a point of contact and my head paid the price. I feared a concussion. Luckily, the Thursday rained and jump 5 was delayed until Friday. Load up and take off; I got on the plane first, which seated me forward in the "Stick." "Go!" The aftermost jumper went out first, and by the time I got to the door the plane had overshot the DZ. A ham fist grabbed my harness and said, "Take a seat, Captain (Army equivalent of Navy Lieutenant two-bar), we're going around." Swell, my first solo jump. Stand up, stand in the door, go!" *Swoosh*, out I went. Pants fluttering, DZ clear, gentle wind, a sure shot not to miss Alabama. Ka-thump! Down for five! Got my wings, and we were going home Saturday.

Social notes: Benning had vacated the First Calvary Division late 1965 and was pretty nearly a ghost town. A cousin of mine was a lieutenant-colonel who was deployed. I had their address and enjoyed a meal one Saturday. Another weekend, I rented a car and drove to Quitman, Georgia, a couple of hours south of Ft. Benning. My uncle was in the cattle business and, with his family, had a farm in Quitman. Three hours down, overnight, three miles back to school. The entire three weeks was a whirl. Apart from the headaches, it wasn't particularly demanding, and nobody quit or was let go—as far as I recall. Regretfully, I suspect some of the boys' names ended up on Jan Scruggs' Washington Vietnam Wall.

Back in Coronado, we had one month to continue preparations for deployment. Our C.O., LCDR Olson, was leading the team west. My first week back I made my first team parachute jump, a night jump near South Bay, San Diego. Another milestone, this time with steerable parachutes, which the teams pioneered. Soft landing on recently-plowed damp sod. Then the other rigors of keeping up qualifications—diving and rifle range. (Those days we spent little time compared with the thousands of training rounds expended today.)

Pre-deployment work-up completed, guys were on half days for a week before mounting out at North Island Naval Air Station (NAS) for our fifty-three-hour prop-driven airlift to the Philippines via Hawaii, Midway, Guam . . . into Cubi Point, next door to the Subic Bay Naval Station, both leased from the Philippines. (Clark Air Force Base, outside Angeles City, was an hour north.) We were a mere forty-eight hours in Subic when the team boarded an advanced operations personnel ship, The U.S.S. Weiss (APD-135), built from a destroyer hull to transport Marines and UDT in advance of an amphibious operation. We were to participate with Marine Recon in operation JACKSTAY, south of Saigon in the *Rung Sat Special Zone,* March 26–April 6, 1966, three days steaming from Subic. The operation was one of a series of amphibious landings aimed at intercepting Viet Cong units operating near the coast. The first tactical effort was led by me with six Frogmen in an IBS onto the perspective beach and guide in the Marine landing unit. It was a seven-mile paddle. We hit the first sand a half-mile offshore at 0200, a very shallow beach slope. Fortunately, the beach was wide and empty, so we settled down to await the Marine arrival at 0600. At the appointed time, Marines waded ashore. "Hi, ya guys!" We immediately waded out with our IBS for the hump back to Diachenko, having accomplished nothing of tactical significance. That same evening opportunity awaited us. Four-man teams inserted fifty yards apart on the north bank of a river beyond the landing zone with the mission of reporting any VC movement— not to shoot unless in clear superior numbers.

Around 1700, twelve teams (UDT and USMC) loaded into whale boats and inserted at low tide. The entire region was tidal! Some teams had water up to their wastes. My group was lucky and stayed dry. Mosquitos are thicker because they are closer to the ground, the solution was to remain upright. One team engaged a junk boat sometime around midnight, past the area curfew—four KIA.

Another team evaded an armed gaggle of men and successfully evaded. How to report? The radios were flooded. Two tides later, around 1000 the next morning, our extraction ride appeared. (We were the farthest upstream and maybe the reason we weren't flooded.) The stupid cammy uniforms we wore—one night—were in tatters. Worse, the ship's showers crapped out; we had to drive boats to the amphibs to wash up. Amazing. But ops continued with several riverine ambushes. We asked the amphibious force staff for some overhead photography on the river and were told 10,000 feet was all they had. Super! Photos couldn't identify outcroppings of sand or sunken logs or what was covered up by fauna (palm leaves, etc.). We were blind. A week more of this nonsense and we were released to return to Subic Bay where we continued standard training operations—small units tactics (mush ignored on the home strand), underwater demolitions, diving, some small arms visits to the Subic range, jungle survival training taught by the native residents, and a few water jumps.

We had basically three assigned detachments to fill: the Amphibious Ready Group (ARG), the assigned diesel submarine (capable of bottoming), and Danang (Frogville Vietnam). The ARG was primarily to the Marines for hydrographic reconnaissance. The "Sub De" for advance beach recon. Danang for mostly are a demolition work, as required. We were due to rotate home in September. Our relief was Underwater Demolition Team TWELVE (UDT-12). I was rather shocked and amazed that several months after our return, I saw the turnover letter written by UDT-12 that our preparation for turnover was near non-existent. I took immediate umbrage and so briefed the new team C.O. "Pappy" Laws. Every officer in charge of a team detachment personally briefed their incoming relief. We took the Sub Det people onboard the boat to demonstrate the rigging of rubber boats as well as diving chamber activation. To add punctuation to my disclaimer, we had to leave our senior cartographer, Second Class Petty Officer L.L. Jones "Double L" to this day, with Team TWELVE because they hadn't trained anyone. Water under the proverbial bridge.

Once back in Coronado, within two months, actually, we learned we would be returning to WESTPAC in February. This news lit a light in the command. That meant, basically, a "port and starboard" rotation—six out, six in. "Ready, get set, go! . . . again." Vietnam in 1967 was getting serious. We had not heard—myself not until two decades later—that the Army had fought a massive battle at Ia Drang. And about this time, SEAL Team ONE was opening for volunteers, which left our group commander, Captain Phil Bucklew, to pronounce, "Once a volunteer, always a volunteer." This meant a draft from the four national UDTs, which generated a good deal of angst in the ranks. Fortunately, discontent remained verbal and mostly everyone who was accepted into the two SEAL teams performed superbly.

Deployment prep was hindered by the lack of adequate funding. One example: we (Team 11) needed two Evenrude outboard engines for our IBS. No funding available at the time; it was months before we got motors. After we were deployed, the team headquarters was ordered to relocate to Okinawa; part of an expansion experiment I was told. The C.O. went north, I stayed as officer in charge in Subic Bay. Ops continued. One interesting thing did happen because of Okinawa. Seven of up got to attend the Army Special Forces Military Freefall course. Quickly, this was an intensive course that resulted in twenty freefall parachuting jumps mostly all in full equipment with oxygen masks. We jumped Wednesdays and both weekend days. We jumped onto a small farming island off Okinawa called Ia Shima. Jumps progressed from an initial five-second delay (one jump) to twenty (one), thirty to sixty, the majority. Our graduation high altitude jump occurred over Taiwan from 20,000 feet at dusk. I think I could see the mainland. I know I experienced three weather layers on the way to 4,000 pull altitude—16,000 foot freefall, landing in a sugarcane field. I packed my chute in a bag, goggles and O2 mask dangling from my helmet. I emerged onto a highway and was surrounded by astonished citizens with their bicycles. It took us over an hour to collect everyone in the local rendezvous saloon to await the bus. And the beer was cold! After leaving the C-130 tailgate, I never saw anyone until I got to the bar! It was a survival jump. Safety first.

After winning the friendship of the Army Jump School administrators, we worked a deal whereby we could train a new platoon of Frogmen in static line basic parachuting to win Army wings. We had admin riggers and training cadre in Subic who would use the Army training syllabus, all under oversight of the Jump School administration. It worked, we taught our own guys, and we used our own "Seven Panel TU" steerable parachutes, as opposed to Army TU-10s. The course took two weeks compared to Ft. Bennings's three. And we didn't have to learn airborne songs. We put a dozen Frogmen through Army-monitored basic jump course. The UDT cadre did a bang-up job keeping the new guys safe in the air.

Our 1967 deployment was nearing a termination point that November. All detachments were assembled in Subic the first week of December for another turnover with UDT-12, which went a lot smoother than the previous one. The team C.O., LCDR Bob Condon, was again on site. We had just completed some surface recons of the Vietnamese IV Corps (southern Vietnam). I had assigned Lieutenant Mike Collins to take his platoon and conduct the daylight reconnaissances. Did a bang-up job operating from U.S.S. Weiss (APD-135). I briefed LCDR Condon on our nine-month deployment and told him I operated by assigning lieutenants with their platoons to operational assignments—like Collins to IV Corps surveys. But my advice was not taken, and the very next morning he departed Subic and started running operations himself. Bob was later killed leading an element on a riverine mission to test out a new mobility swimmer device. Seems to me the place to "test" new river toys is in Mississippi, not the combat zone.

Deployment responsibility ended, we were holding for homeward transport and lollygagged a few days at the gym, on ref-dives, packing. A helicopter became free, so we thought we would benefit from one more training jump before Christmas. We had a couple of freefall rigs at the unit; rigger Al Schmize and I figured we would freefall. We got out a t 12,500 feet AGL (Above Ground Level) going for a standard pull altitude of 4,000 feet. (I hadn't yet become so comfortable with the U.S. Parachute Associate standard of 2,500-foot pull altitude.) Jump went without issue until I landed on a rock, tearing my ankle ligaments! I saw the bone pushing a lump in my jump boot and hammered it back in place with a single smack—so far no pain. Immediate chopper ride to the Cubi Point Naval Hospital. This was December 12, they had to wait for the swelling to subside and operated a couple days later. Leg cast from my left ankle to halfway up my thigh. The doc told me they cast past the next successive joint, knee in my case. I was stuck in Cubi over Christmas and was finally moved to Clark Air Force Base on New Year's Eve. The C-141 transport was crammed with real wounded from Vietnam. Air Force nurses did a fantastic job taking care of the guys. We flew into Guam to refill when in a commotion I looked up into the face of comedian Bob Hope whose troop was concluding another holiday combat visit to deployed military bases. He shook hands with all who could or were not sleeping. I recall lying at the Cubi Hospital reading a book of John Steinbeck press releases from World War II through Korea and then Vietnam. Steinbeck lauded Hope's efforts to bring a piece of home to the several combat zones. Hope mentioned to me that his son at that time was in San Diego.

It was an auspicious occasion to see the great man in the flesh . . . you couldn't miss him!

I got back to San Diego and the Balboa Naval Medical Center on crutches, and would be for six weeks. I wanted out, I needed to get back to UDT-11 before orders could be cut whereby I would lose my executive officer slot. I could hobble, read message traffic, write fitness reports, and carry out a plan of the day on restricted duty. I was fortunately able to return to the command before too long— or wasn't missed. They were still winding down from deployment and relaxed holiday routine, which wrapped up around the second week of January. I was assigned a room at the Amphibious Base Bachelor Officer Quarters (BOQ) pending locating an apartment in Coronado, which happily came about in two days' search—711 7th Street. I think it was with furniture. My job was secure, and I could concentrate on healing. Late February, the two pins in my ankle were removed in the doctor's office, and I was looking at a couple more weeks for the "holes" to heal and the repaired ligament could stand walking pressure—and later running and fin kicking. By late March 1968 I was swimming with the team, slow running, and finally cured of crutches.

Then I got orders to the Surface Ship Department Head School at Newport, Rhode Island, to report late July. A new challenge, but first UST-11 was looking forward to an Operational Readiness Inspection (ORI) in mid-June. These are opportunities to shine—"all hands on deck." We were still in a minor deployment mindset; everyone was current with equals; manning wasn't as yet debilitated by a SEAL team draft. We could perform and do well functionally. My challenge was crafting an Operations Order (OPORD) that would exercise most of the Required Operational Capabilities (ROC) of a UDT. We were assigned the availability of an LST (Landing

Ship, Tank) for five days. My plan was to establish San Clemente Island Training Area for the ORI region. Areas were designated for land warfare attacks, hinterland recons, and the standard bread and butter UDT mission, beach demo clearance. The resulting OPORD was six inches thick with a half dozen special operations "missions." SEAL Team ONE land graders sat in on all briefings and judged the performance of the platoons. To sum up, all demolition explosions went "high order" on fussed demolitions. I went two days without sleep until FINEX was declared. I checked out with the C.O., LT Weyers, and hit the unrumpled rack for the six hours transit back to San Diego. By mid-July I was a "short-timer." Bags packed into my car, checked out of the apartment, gassed up, I headed east, first to visit my parents in Tucson a couple of days before the five-day trek to New England.

What'd I learn? How to assign people. In two years on the team as operations and executive officer, the most important thing I learned was assigning the right mix of people to operations—in addition to pre-planning. This meant affording platoon level officers the opportunity to lead their men. Next, make sure the technical makeup of operational elements had the right technicians assigned. This required the input of senior enlisted leaders. Command Master Chief Harry Tindall was instrumental in assuring the right people were available. He was indispensable; the chiefs as a group were indispensable—several with long-standing UDT experience stemming from WW II and Korea. (Timewise, 1945 to 1965 was only twenty years.) But I had learned this lesson as an ensign in the fleet four years earlier when I tried doing the Division Chief's job, and the kindly old salt sagely reminded me how the Navy worked. I had a long way to go in the service and that advice stood me in good stead throughout.

Summer in Subic Bay, The Philippines.

CHAPTER 7

DESTROYER SCHOOL—OFF TO SEA AGAIN

Cross-country treks are part of naval service. I had just completed three assignments in San Diego since graduation from the Naval Academy in 1961—Halsey Powel, Cruiser-Destroyer Flotilla 7, and UDT-11. In the sixties, there were scarce career opportunities in Underwater Demolition. There was no designation of "Naval Special Warfare." Officers aspiring of a naval career were always exhorted to get back to sea; a tour or two in UDT was tolerated instead of a shore duty assignment, but promotion up the career ladder depended on shipboard performance. My time to get back to sea had come. Vietnam to a great extent drove the creation of a Naval Special Warfare community, which Navy recognized in 1970 by establishing official officer/enlisted career paths. So August 1968 found me re-entering the Surface Warfare community. There were no Surface Warfare breast insignia or formal acknowledgement of the community until Admiral Elmo Zumwalt, fresh from Vietnam and Chief of Naval Operations (CNO) created them.

"Destroyer School," the informal cognomen for Surface Warfare Department Head School, was established to polish the Surface community, like Submarine School. I reported to Halsey Powel fresh out of USNA—three summer Midshipmen summer cruises under my belt. Otherwise totally green. Department head had by then achieved professional status within the fleet. Orders depended on graduation from the course. Simply put, it was a service attempt to stiffen the performance and polish of surface officers. I would judge that it worked; all shipboard junior officers recognized they had to pass the court for any career chance. I suspect it worked.

Newport, Rhode Island, is a magical place! The people are delightful; the lobsters are unequalled; the weather can be a challenge. Winters are cruel. Summers are cooled by offshore breezes. Fall is majestic, and everybody looks forward to spring. Newport used to be a major Navy homeport. The end of Vietnam basically ended Newport's importance with the exception of the Naval War College and sundry schools, of which department head was significant. There used to be a legal school there; don't know if it still exists—I made a lasting friend there, a Marine lawyer, whom I still encounter in San Diego.

Destroyer School lasts six months. I started Class 35 in August, and we graduated early February. I had orders to U.S.S. Strong (DD-758), homeported in Charleston, South Carolina. I drove out of Newport that February in unbelievably mild weather. Headed south to New York City to visit friends. I got there early Friday and it was promenade weather. I awoke early Saturday morning at 6:30; baseball snowflakes were falling Pell Mell on the city. "General quarters!" Get outta town fast or resolve to stay until Easter. Which way—south via Lincoln Tunnel or north to George Washington Bridge. I opted for the southern escape. Cars all over the highway, some in gutters, several catawampus on the road, no lessening of snowfall . . . for as far as vision permitted. Windfall for the tow companies. The snow continued until I came out of the tunnel into Delaware where it slackened. I was enroute to Little Creek, Virginia, and the home of Tom Nelson. Whew! Disaster avoided.

Before reporting into Charleston, there were a few groups in Destroyer School. This was not a senior officer course. It was strictly "nuts n' bolts" engineering subjects: the power plant, gunnery, electronics, communications, navigation. The destroyer electrical system: final exam was to reproduce a destroyer electrical system upside down and backward! This was a grunt course throughout. This course was all about what happened after the "start button" was pressed. And who among us could ever forget the World War II film about cleaning boiler firesides as the Newport fall sun was ducking below the Friday main mast? The course afforded a ten-day at-sea cruise each class. We joined in with an ongoing fleet exercise with a weekend in Puerto Rico.

Weekends were free. In my case, I elected to drive to western Massachusetts to skydive. I would leave the apartment at 0600 and arrive at the drop zone at 0900; throw out three parachute jumps, chug a beer, and wolf a short dinner, and get back home by 9:00 PM. Sunday was homework, period. There were some infrequent formal affairs to attend, nothing very vigorous. The bars and restaurants in Newport are noteworthy; my favorite remains the Black Pearl—best New England clam chowder in America. And the time period: 1968. "The pill" was altering society. Music was searing the air waves; 1968 Vietnam New Year. "Tet" had altered wartime patience. The movie *Forest Gump* reflected the times like Woodstock. Just about 90 percent of my "DESTECH" classmates were Vietnam vets. We all observed the social changes occurring and yawned. No opportunity for sideburns or beards for us—until Zumwalt okayed them in 1970. We were direct products of the 1950s. One social rule changed as the war progressed:

neckties were on the way out. By the time the official conflict ended in 1975, neckties were history—like the services officers' clubs. Much of society was changing as we contemplated post-war assignments in the coming seventies. I was looking forward to my destroyer duty, never imagining I would have two more Southeast Asia tours to serve.

I reported into USS Strong that February, at the time in dry dock as part of a normal shipyard six-week availability. Shipyard periods permit crew members to attend shore based schools for professional courses on equipment and team training sessions—antisubmarine, anti-air, shore bombardment, etc. They afford opportunity to upgrade equipment—assuming it can be accomplished within scheduled time. The shipyard afforded me time to learn the ship and my operations department personnel. Daily meals were served in the ship's wardroom except dinner as most officers were married; most bachelors lived off ship, too, so the duty officer and whoever was left shared the wardroom.

Shipyard days ended. Strong was refloated and prepared for post-yard shakedown. Minor nicks were noted for follow-up repairs, and ship's company prepared for a commanding officer change of command and refresher training at Guantanamo (GITMO), Cuba. Our new CO was Commander Richard "Dick" Dalla Mura, USN, a 1953 Naval Academy grad. Strong was his fourth (or fifth?) command; he was a consummate mariner and ship handler. We were ensured a stimulating experience in six weeks Refresher Training (REFTRA). In the meantime, we used the time to get to know each other and participate in local fleet exercise that took up to Puerto Rico. This exercise lasted three weeks in late spring. We began final team work-ups before REFTRA.

Underway, our course to Cuba was down the Florida coast. I was able to plot the ship's navigation track off Cape Canaveral during the Apollo 11 moon shot on July 16, 1969, with Armstrong, Collins, and Aldrin. Loud as firecrackers, audible two miles off-shore, and the sparkler exhaust tail was seemingly twice the length of the huge Saturn rocket. We listened to audio piped in over the ship's "1 MC." Wow (a familiar Vietnam-era expletive!) and whew—what a thrill! I can't think of any at-sea experience more stimulating since the Christmas Island nuclear tests I witnessed six years earlier. Well, "stimulating" is a broad category—in my list I could add midnight underway replenishment alongside an oiler, returning to homeport, shore bombardment.

REFTRA is 100 percent drudgery. Every aspect of destroyer employment is exercised. Shipboard warfighting teams are honed to subject matter perfection—or as close as the amount of time provided allows. One area we sucked in was ship boarding and seizure, an emphasized drill following the Cuban missile crisis. Truth is, we never had the time to invest on close combat team maneuvering from the whaleboat to a ship's main deck and clearance of compartments. If a ship offered no resistance, fine. Modern SEAL teams spend days rehearsing ship takedowns. Still, we passed the basics and felt secure with our final war problem performance. We were on our way home. One final comment on REFTRA: the training cadre expects ships entering refresher training to have afforded team members from all departments to have completed the shore school courses applicable to the ship's standing "Rocs and Poes" (Required Operational Capability and Prospective Operational Environment). Op-area expected: Mediterranean, Western Pacific, weather expected, etc. The Combat Information Center (CIC) team should have attended the anti-submarine trainer, shore bombardment, ant-air warfare trainer. All departments in a destroyer has its list of battle bills the general quarters teams need be proficient in.

Back home in Charleston, just before the 1969 Labor Day weekend, it was a welcome stand-down from the summer's operations. Next hurdle: pre-deployment workup for a six-month cruise to the Sixth Fleet (Mediterranean). To say the least, it was a frenetic fall trying to achieve 100 percent across the board with crew members possessing the correct "NEC" (Navy Enlisted Classification). Shipboard gear requires a trained technician on most equipment. Bad example: Strong had an air search radar— SPS-40. We had one second class (E5) electronics technician with a proper NEC. This was an impressive radar provided one could keep it running. It was a Philco product. We were able to keep it running thirty minutes during an entire six-month Med deployment! Every time we tied up in Naples, a Philco tech-rep would come aboard to troubleshoot the radar. We steamed the entire deployment under CASREP (Casualty Report). Ships can CASREP most anything. For example, that following summer we CASREPed for a lack of NECs. CASREPs get briefed to the Chief of Naval Operations (CNO) every day, from a carrier right down to a mine ship. The summer of 1970 was a trying period, about which more later.

First stop in "Med" was Gibraltar, a huge rock overlooking the western entrance to the Mediterranean and a burr in the Spanish saddle owing to its English ownership. We refueled then to Naples, Italy, the Navy "hitching post" for the Sixth Fleet. First order of business was attendance at the Squadron Commander's briefing with Sixth Fleet staffers. We got running orders, exercise schedules, maintenance dates, port visit approval, and importantly, which destroyers would make Black Sea transits to exercise Freedom of the Sea. Strong was scheduled for two transits, which perforce caused our presence in Athens, Greece, for thirty days—two two-week availabilities in Piraeus, the port city for Athens. It was an uptight period for the

Greeks; Army colonels had taken over the country. Piraeus hosted a British watering hole called John Bull, which hosted cold beer and darts; it was a favorite joint of the crew and walking distance to the ship. For my part, the area was fine for jogging, and I would lope over to the Greek Naval Academy swimming pool after work. I was able to continue my shipboard physical activity. Stemming from my earlier shipboard duty—Halsey Powel and CRUDESFLOT 7—I devised an exercise routine of dynamic intensity, especially trying underway with ship rolls: ten sets of ten interrelated, twenty-five prone flutter kicks, twenty-five squat jumps in two minutes. I was breathing hard. The easier workout was jogging/swimming—less stressful, which is not to intimate that running and swimming are not energetic. I know them both intimately. My disappointment was not being able to interest any shipmates to join me. It got humorous over dinner in the wardroom; I invited all takers to join in. My CIC officer did challenge me to a five-mile run in our next port of call, Valencia, Spain, if I remember correctly. I gave him a handicap: I would run in jump boots, which gave my reconstructed ankle better support weight notwithstanding. I won. Ho hum. (Truth end, the C.O. asked me to lighten up on my subordinate. "Aye, aye, Sir!") But back to Greece. We accumulated a month in Athens, entertained several bartenders, and fell in love with the fried chicken livers served atop the Athens Hilton. We were fortunate to spend 1970 New Year's Eve in port Athens. We were poised to go into the Black Sea with all due trepanation; we had visions of another *Pueblo* event when that U.S. Navy ship was captured by North Korea. The OPORDER for each of our thee-day transits was five feet long! Air Force and Navy aircraft were on-call. I always had my doubts how long it would take an Air Force jet to make it to the Black Sea. In the event, the Black Sea is aptly named; it's pitch. Within an hour of our entry into the Black Sea we were escorted—shadowed, actually—by a Soviet Riga destroyer. They stuck around about a day—got close one time about a hundred yards off our port (left) side; they were interested. The thing that impressed me was the acceleration the Soviet ship exhibited with her turbine engines. At that time the Soviets had better missiles too. We were about a decade behind with our Burke Class. (I was in the Pentagon fall 1979 and observed the dedication the Surface Warfare Directorate exhibited in support of the new class—to get it commissioned before "the ole gentlemen" passed from the scene. They made it.) Happily, our two patrols were uneventful—grey days, chilly nights, black water. The nearest we came to real excitement was steaming down the Sea of Mamara (past Istanbul) in a fog. We took some heat for going close and anchoring until the fog lifted. The "squad dog" said we had no clearance to anchor. I was not privy to Captain Dalla Mura's conversation beyond his recounting. Safety first—something about the old adage, "Constant vigilance is the price of safe navigation."

The cruise offered great opportunities to exercise all the fleet events: nighttime refueling from an oiler and carrier, hour-long daylight alongside replenishment drills, great port visits beyond Athens and Naples, to wit: Valencia—my run and the opportunity to use my Berlitz Spanish on guided ship tours with Spanish school kids. And a unique couple of guitar lessons with a Flamenco guitarist. I loved the instrument, still do except for arthritis in my fingers (and great reverence for Django Reinhardt). Flamenco is alive and well in Spain, a vestige of Moorish legacy, which carried on after Isabella and Ferdi kicked them out. But one most impressive example of ship handling happened in Genoa, Italy; after dark, in a drizzle, Captain Dalla Mura took the sea detail (a formal assigned station for hands) "deck con" and pivoted the Strong into a stern to "Med Moor"—bow pointed out to sea in case of an emergency Cold War dispersal. His maneuver without a tugboat was most impressive—the luster of which has not dimmed with me since I observed it as the Sea Detail Officer of the deck! If my Captain "D" ever read these lines, he should know I hold him in the highest regard, not just from ship driving, but by his constant example of cheerful excellence.

We returned to Charleston just before Memorial Day weekend. Charleston has a tropical climate; it was in full swing as we chugged up the Cooper River—an hour-and-a-half sea detail along a twisting (treacherous, with sand dunes, tides, wind, and traffic) narrow course; passing traffic was akin to playing "chicken" with ships and barges. I almost needed a shower after every transit! The Mediterranean in late spring is not warm, nor is the Atlantic. Coming home we picked up nearly ten degrees of latitude below "Gib." You knew you were "home" when the local gulls fell. I astern of the ship for mess deck delicacies. Sea Detail was set by the time we passed—not "hit"— the Charleston sea buoy, and an hour-plus later the band could be heard. Next challenge was preparing to weather the new Chief of Naval Operations, Admiral Elmo Zumwalt. Briefly, he was recently Commander Naval Forces Vietnam and was selected by President Nixon over many senior admirals. That summer, the Navy was to undergo a tectonic cultural shift. Beards were allowed and a snow storm of CNO "Z-Grams" micromanaged the service. More, Zumwalt started laying up and decommissioning various older ships; Zumwalt was later to boast that he sank more Navy ships than the Imperial Japanese Navy. Effect on Strong: we became a reserve training ship. Late that summer Commander Dalla Mura got new orders to a surface staff, and I started on my third commanding officer. It was time to bolt graciously.

I was a new lieutenant commander (04) and was offered orders as operations officer with Naval Special Warfare Group (Vietnam), which position accelerated to Executive Officer on detachment of the incumbent. The officer-in-charge was Commander Dave Del Giudice, the first C.O. of SEAL Team ONE (1962–1964). The group was assigned to the Operational Control (OPCON) of Commander U.S. Naval Forces Vietnam—formerly commanded by Zumwalt. The SpecWar staff's main job was to oversee operations of deployed SEAL Teams and Special Boats. But let us review my return to Naval Special Warfare in a chapter of its own. My Surface Warfare career was ending.

What'd I learn from two years on Strong? First, fleet operations and administration of a department, which meant digesting sundry operations orders and being forehanded preparing the department for exercise and missions. Formation steaming is learned by doing hours and days of round-the-clock bridge watches. From REFTRA drills, doing movement solutions with grease pencils had become routine. Anticipation was the internal acclamation of shipboard culture and behavior. The adage, "A taunt ship is a happy ship" meant respect for ship's bills (rules); another: "Constant vigilance is the price of safe navigation." Both adages apply across most Navy assignments, and from my 1957 Plebe Year "Reef Points":

> "Now these are the laws of the Navy,
> Unwritten and varied they be;
> And he who is wise will observe them, Going
> down in his ship to the sea."

It was time to go back to the war zone . . .

OFFICER OF THE DECK, USS STRONG (DD-758) somewhere in
the Mediterranean, winter 1969–70; I had recently pinned on Lieutenant
Commander rank. Destroyer School doesn't provide opportunity for
photographs. Underway Navy shots have been adequately displayed in
VICTORY AT SEA.

CHAPTER 8

BACK TO THE WAR: A YEAR IN SAIGON (1971-72)

My orders to Saigon for a yearlong tour arrived at Strong late November 1970 to report to the staff of the Commander U.S. Naval Forces Vietnam (COMNAVFORV) in February. I detached from the ship mid-December and reported for interim duty with Commander Naval Special Warfare Group ONE (COMNAVSPECWARGRU ONE) for briefings and updates on SEAL/Special Boat deployments. I met several officers with recent combat experience that was invaluable. I wouldn't land completely cold, although I was soon to realize I had a lot to learn. But it's pretty much that way with every new set of orders and assignments. Coming up to speed with a good attitude is critical, that is, listen to everybody. I was there as the specific relief of Lieutenant Commander Walt Otte, a Korean War frogman. Our officer-in-charge (OIC) was Commander Dave Del Giudice, the first commanding officer of SEAL Team ONE—great leader with an uncanny ability to navigate the many NAVFORV directorates. Political acumen counts in massive military staffs!

Saigon working hours were seven to seven, seven days a week—calculated to wear everybody out, except for our in-country ally, the Vietnam Army, never paid much attention to American workaholics. U.S. Navy SEALs deployed as platoons of twelve men, two officers and ten enlisted men. In early 1971, we were fielding some six platoons throughout the Vietnamese Delta south of Saigon (IV CORPS—"Four Corps"). The major occupation-mission emphasis of SEALs at that time was interdicting the Viet Cong infrastructure, which basically devolved into capturing senior VC, and ultimately destroy the VC as an effective combat organization. Here, with the benefit of hindsight, one can only muse on the potential of a political settlement of the war—way above the paygrades of NAVSPECWARGU (Vietnam) sailors.

Deployed SEAL platoons were fielded from both east and west coast teams, ONE and TWO. Both sources boasted exceptional combat records. Regretfully, many guys were killed and wounded and were having an impact on the enemy. "Men with green faces" was a VC cognomen for SEALs. One of my old UDT-11 teammates deployed as Platoon Commander ZULU Platoon was Lieutenant Mike Collins. We deployed together during 1967; Mike handled IV Corps beach recons. We attended freefall (HALO) school in Okinawa that year—a lively break in the deployment; we made our first jumps together. We had swum together at the Naval Academy—he on the Plebe team; I was on the varsity, four years senior (Mike was a Plebe in the Class of 1964). Mike was a later team captain and a 1964 Olympic Trials contestant in the 100-meter freestyle (finishing fourth). I later saw him in UDTRA when I was XO of Team ELEVEN. Hoo yah! That March Mike was up briefing CDR

Del Giudice on Delta ops out of Ben Tre. That Sunday evening, Mike and I shared dinner; he was returning to his platoon that Monday morning. He was killed on a riverine operation that Wednesday morning, the victim of a VC grenade attack on his boat. He was killed on the spot. Commander Del Giudice ordered the platoon to stand down—based on cumulative losses and wounds. Collins was posthumously awarded the Silver Star. He was one of the best respected officers in SEAL Team ONE. Seven years later (1978), I initiated a proposal to name the newly-renovated Coronado Amphibious Base pool, which was approved and inaugurated with a ceremony headed by Vice Admiral Saint George, Commander Pacific Fleet Surface Ship Command. Mike's name is joined by all the other SEALs killed in action in Vietnam is on the Wall in Washington, D. C.

Collin's death occurred two months into my year-long tour. Operations continue. Naval Special Warfare Detachment ("Det") GOLF was stationed south of Saigon tasked with coordinating Direct Action (DA) missions, largely oriented against the VC leadership (as mentioned previously). Liaison with Vietnamese Navy SEALS was the responsibility of "Det" SIERRA. It was regretted that too often the Viet SEALs were called on as presidential bodyguards. Such a price to pay for elitism when your country is trying to develop democracy—well . . . ahem.

If anyone cares to remember 1971, go and Google the year. I remember Nixon taking us off the Gold Standard . . . and prices skyrocketed. The cost of the Porsche TARGA I ordered before leaving home went up a couple of grand. (The dealership was nice enough to split the difference!) The biggest military policy shift was called "Vietnamization,"—"Word" just asked me if I wanted to add it to the dictionary. The thrust was to turn the war over to the Vietnamese generals along with the sundry bases and logistics facilities. This was summer 1971. James Taylor—still darling of the left—was regaling us with "You've Got a Friend." "Just yesterday morning . . ." I had the tape in my office, and a photo of a Porsche. Just this year (2015) Taylor was flown to London by the State Department to help harmonize foreign policy. Maybe he should have gone to Hanoi?

For us in NSWGRU Saigon, Vietnamization was the signal to start rolling back VCI (Viet Cong Interdiction) Direct Action platoon drama. And do what? Recon river buoys? Move to pure reconnaissance missions? Like patrolling the outskirts of villages and report any suspicious enemy activity to . . . Police Special Branch, ARV, MACV? It was clearly time to recast SEAL team employment and shift more emphasis onto our Viet Navy counterparts, the "LDNN" (*Lien Doc Ngnoi Nhia* "soldiers who fight under the sea"—elegant, or not). Regardless of their past performance, they were getting the shtick. This was the direction we were headed by summer's end, approved by COMNAVFORV and MACV. The trick was to relay the decision back to the States to alter training to emphasize reconnaissance and training/advisory tasks. It was a very difficult transition after four years of essentially "bang and burn." Like kicking in hooch doors, and capturing VC. But the rules of engagement (ROE) were changing too, for example, "don't shoot unless being shot at"—nowhere stated so but interpreted that way. Helicopters had to be taking dings to the fuselage before returning fire. On the rivers, same applied: no more "recon by fire" or "free fire zones." 50-caliber machine guns were especially dangerous by dint of range. And "death" by U.S. had to be supported by evidence, like one SEAL op resulted in a Viet girl taken under fire when she burst from a structure running. NAVFORV sent a JAG officer back to the village for depositions of the action. (Lucky they weren't ambushed!) We had clearly overstayed our time.

At this point, Dave Del Giudice had been relieved by Commander Dave Schaible, "Uncle Dave." The LDNN headquarters had relocated to Cat Lai, a former French Navy base thirty minutes south of Saigon. We were to relocate too, so we split duty at Cat Lai and NFV. The major task was to prepare the LDNN for follow-on employment—organization, infrastructure, and equipment. "Uncle Sugar" was paying for this stuff so we had to prepare a Program Objective Document (POM) just like the States—it was the only model naval officers had. (Duh!) Guns and personal gear were easy: get the sizes right—all "small." Next was the outfitting of a riverine force, particularly the heavy landing craft—"Landing Craft, Medium, (LCM)" that needed to be fit with ground tackle, comm gear, guns, and armament—no small task as funds had to be identified and (yep) paid for. This was our staffing imperative by year's end. And it had to capture Vietnamese approval even though they weren't paying for it. Go figure. But we had witnessed the pillage of Vietnamese bases during Vietnamization and were adamant Cat Lai and LDNN assets would be safe guarded . . . for a while, anyway. Cat Lai was looking good. (Fast forward to 1973, when I had occasion to revisit Saigon following a trip to Phnom Penh. Cat Lai had regressed to pre-'72 conditions. Goats were in the hangars, grass uncut, swimming pool clogged with algae, chickens clucking in the front lawn . . . I will revisit later. The end was just two years ahead.)

Two lighthearted stories during the year that were memorable. While assigned to Saigon, Americans were eligible to join the French *Circle Sportif*, a center-city athletic and social club. It boasted a thirty-five meter swimming pool, a dozen tennis courts, and an okay weigh room (with barbells dating to 1925!). It was located a block away from NAVFORV and our headquarters. I met several French officials and one, a doctor, Henri Pelloux, remained a friend until his passing away. I would visit him in Paris. The summer before my orders to Phnom Penh, 1974, he came to California and we enlisted him for our Masters Swimming Club relay team for the Long Course Championships in Santa Clara. Great fun. We had swum together during my time in Saigon and through him I met a French clique at *Circle Sportif*—great opportunity to catch up on my laggard spoken French. One day, the French Council General, Jacques de Folin, lost his bridge in the pool. I jumped into the *picine* to "recon" the bottom for some "teeth." Found 'em on the third dive! Welcome to the inner circle. He had a Christmas Eve dinner (1971) to which I was the only American present in my resplendent tropical whites. The meal was served in quarters for about eighteen of us. Later, late January, I held a dinner for my French acquaintances at Restaurant La Cave (my favorite), de Folin attended. Several years later, he sent me a copy of his 1993 Vietnam history, *Indochine, 1940-1955, Le fin d'un live*, inscribed, "For admiral George Worthington with fond memories of the pool in Saigon." (Folin was a 1939 French Naval Academy grad who migrated to French Foreign Affairs and served as Consul General in Saigon with rank of ambassador and later as ambassador to Jordan, Athens, and Dublin.) I had my boss, Schaible, and relief, Tommy Nelson, and an old Army pal from Brown University, Scott McGurk, along too. And the McGurk entry tops off my assignment in Saigon. One evening in mid-January, I and a couple of staff pals walked into Mimi's Bar in center Saigon. I had never been there the entire year. There at the bar was McGurk! I hadn't seen him since June 1957, after our freshman year at Brown. Turns out I matriculated to the Naval Academy and McGurk to

West Point. I graduated with the Class of 1961; Scott had a run in with "German" and turned back a year graduating with West Point 1962—from which class he attended Ranger School with classmate General Wayne Downing, USA (RIP). Scott retired a Special Forces Colonel and attended my son's graduation jump at Fort Benning, Georgia, ten years ago.

I will overlook my two R&R weeks in Hong Kong and Sidney, Australia, except to note meeting one shining light in Hong Kong, the owner of the Godown Bistro, Irishman Bill Nash, who stayed on in Asia after WW II and became a businessman. Godown will energize a lot of speculative misdirection, but in Pidgeon English it means basement. Nash's joint was in a refurbished basement, ergo the name. The last time I saw Nash was 1995, when I made two trips to Vietnam. Google announces the Godown closed in 1998 after several eras serving British and Yank servicemen.

My year in Saigon ended with a walk down the "yellow brick lane." Literally, yellow footprints walking to the urination stop for drug testing before getting on the aircraft. It's hazy today, if that walk took place days or hours before taking off. What are they gonna do, turn the plane around at Guam? Think about it: several flights a day of troops returning home; how long does it take to change colors in a P-vial? One medic/corpsman for each plane or a host of tinkle testers? Anyway, I unsurprisingly passed, was packed, and had orders to command SEAL Team ONE that March. We landed to cheers of glee at Travis Air Force Base, northwest of San Francisco. But to San Francisco Airport and on to San Diego to check in before heading to Tucson—family and new Porsche. Truth be known, no one spit on me at the airport, nor did I ever see it, though I have no reason to contradict anyone. It was February and the snow at Aspen was calling its tropical disciple. A few days disrupting parents then off in new car to Colorado with James Taylor warming the Porsche Targa interior! With new ski boots and a pair of Red Star skies way longer than I needed—who knew then that short skies were more sensible. Downsizing the ski length market would take thirty years. I later checked into SEAL Team ONE as relief for Lieutenant Commander Dan Hendrickson. Our change of command was March 17, 1972. I had a lot to learn!

What'd I learn on the Saigon staff? Primarily I learned to identify the staff section with the most influence on our issues. This isn't to suggest schmoozing, but it does mean to route Point Papers through (or "To") the operative action officer and not bypass any with collateral interest. Snuffing the chain has an immediate impact on whatever support you might need, be it operational approval or funding. Now, this is not intended as a philosophical or ideological posture; it's purely a cornerstone of adept staff work. I did not have the same lessons learned from my aide tour (COMCRUDESFLOT 7). Pushing action papers up a chain has to be learned firsthand—by doing. The year 1971 was my tenth year of service, and the staffing procedures I incorporated in Saigon were part of every follow-on assignment, including the Pentagon.

MY YEAR IN SAIGON

Home to Tucson after a year in Saigon—nothing a new 1972 Porsche couldn't cure. Of course the bill went up owing to Nixon scrapping the Gold Standard. The dealership split the delta. That's patriotism!

Mother and me in the Country Club pool. My membership in the Saigon Cercle Sportif went far maintaining sanity and health. I also met some interesting people, mostly French, the French Charge' d'Affaires, Jacque de Folin, who sent me a copy of his Vietnamese history 1940–1955.

CHAPTER 9

SEAL TEAM ONE 1972–1974

St. Patrick's Day 1972, U.S. Naval Amphibious Base, Coronado, California. Muster to quarters for a change of command. Long gone are the days when lieutenants commanded teams—or lieutenant commanders. To call it "grade creep" would, today, be wrong. Teams today are basically twice plus the size of sixties teams. SEAL teams ONE and TWO were commissioned with lieutenant COs. All teams today are full commanders. Lieutenant commanders lead operational elements, not so in the early seventies. Naval Special Warfare had no flag officers until 1974 when "Irish" Fynn was selected. Let me note an opinion here: as the first active duty, non-Reserve Officer, flag select, Flynn was screwed by the Navy when he was not assigned as first commander of the Naval Special Warfare Command. This is not a slight against Rear Admiral Chuck Le Moyne, who was a superb officer and our second flag officer, but he could have waited a couple of years. So why not? Dunno and probably never will; doubt even Irish has a clue. Politics? Hmmm.

Former Secretary of the Navy John Lehman told me (many years later) his urging the selection board to seek a SEAL admiral, and is quoted therewith in our 2012 photo-anthology Naval Special Warfare/Navy SEAL Teams. More on SEAL flag officers. In 1991 Chief of Naval Operations, Frank Kelso, told me he didn't think our community size needed more than one two-star. Today, we have thirteen!

Taking over a Navy command is an onerous responsibility. I learned very early in my shipboard duty the role of Navy Chief Petty Officers (CPO), to wit: use them in the chain of command relative to the sailors. In the 1970s SEAL teams most chiefs had several combat deployments ... and weren't to be toyed with running their platoons and departments. Most CPOs in teams ONE and TWO had over twenty years' experience—decades more than their platoon commanders. This was an experienced cohort of warfighters. That reality obtains to this day; and many have college degrees. The Naval Special Warfare Center advises that clearly a third of incoming volunteers have degrees.

The era folding in upon Naval Special Warfare—SEAL and Underwater Demolition Teams—was one of clear and distinct cuts. In December 1971, the last remaining Direct Action SEAL platoons departed Vietnam. One platoon was assigned to Naval Special Warfare Unit ONE in Subic Bay, Philippines. Underwater Demolition Teams continued support of the Amphibious Ready Groups (ARG) in the Mediterranean and Far West. That's not very many when you consider SEAL Team had a "purple" mission requirement—that is, they were eligible for joint assignment by Commander in Chief Pacific. This joint duty posture was somehow hard to explain to the Seventh Fleet staff, who saw all Navy units "theirs." This dichotomy of duty was clearer to me some years later as Group Commander. In 1972, the duty was protecting force levels and eek out employment—opportunities and, ready your paycheck, employment.

In all the administrative chaos, the Bureau of Naval Personnel (BUPERS) directed us to eliminate twenty-four billets—service paid spaces on the team. This edict was reflected by our group commander to be complied with. "The buck stops here." How to do it gently? No way. I elected to cut from new accessions from training, all without deployment; "new guys," in essence. They would be made available to their rating detailers for shipboard assignments with opportunity to come back in after the drawdown was over. I was, in retrospect, insensitive in not announcing it to the people involved collectively and the team community at large. I'm sure everybody knew the deal, but there are characteristics of leadership which I was to learn are often more sensitive than I was capable of at the time. Presumably, I learned with some coaching from senior enlisted SEALs and was able to "lead" three more Naval Special Warfare commands.

One of the esteemed senior SEALs was Senior Chief Petty Officer Claude Willis, an African-American, who was admired and well-liked throughout the team. I learned from him that if a man was comfortable and performing well in an East or West Coast team, why not let him stay—needs of the service considered? At that time an effort was underway to cross-train enlisted with coast-to-coast transfers. Huh? We weren't thinking clearly at the time. Here goes: an enlisted man makes the team cut and deploys several times, maybe marries, has a house mortgage, and a couple of kids in school, wife with a job ... pick up, sell house, rip kids out of school and away from friends, trek cross-country, find quarters. All to satisfy some flesh-molding Navy personnel scheme? Willis had it right. We tried way late to soften the blow. And at what cost to the Navy, for orders and travel expenses? Willis had it right.

One chopping effort was aimed at transitioning SEAL teams to the Naval Reserve. This was about 1973. And at the insisting of one of our own officers. This was nearing the precipice of death knell. There were all sorts of machinations about the livelihood of Naval Special Warfare. What form should the community conform to for future utility? Grade ranks were slowly absorbing promotions. Commander John O'Drain picked up Captain (06), and was assigned to head the SEAL Team, UDTs 11 and 12, and the Coastal Boat units. We're not going to bother with block diagrams of command relationships; suffice it to say, we dodged the "reserve bullet" and survived by the excellent staff work of Commander Ted Growbowski getting the CNO, Admiral Zumwalt, to sign out a letter preserving the two Naval Special Warfare groups (ONE and TWO) which action perforce saved the subordinate commands, that is, saving the groups include the assigned commands. A huge community exhalation was heard coast to coast. "Whew!" We still had a future. In truth, Zumwalt had seen firsthand SEAL team performances in Vietnam. He appreciated the unconventional warfare capability in Naval Special Warfare. He would have loved the bin Laden operation!

Beyond the infighting and budget crunching, we enjoyed the downtime to develop some esoteric training, three kinds worth nods: cold weather (including skiing), sailing, and freefall parachuting. SEAL teams had some "research" latitude in the Required Operational Capabilities (ROC) document and additional correspondence that eludes my memory at the moment. We sent platoons up to Mammoth Mountain for ski instruction. We sent platoons down to the Coronado Navy Sailing Club (operating in San Diego Bay). Skydiving: some guys got to go to Army HALO School, although those billets were tight.

We started our own classes, which were heavily solicited. We were jumping our own rigs. But we were learning. Cold weather training supported PACOM requirements. Sailing could be defended as an insertion platform through indigenous fishing fleets. Freefalling is, today, a required qualification in basic SEAL training, along with static line parachuting. We did it by our bootstraps.

By early 1974 the pressure on manpower was loosening up. Billets were "POMed" and approved for restoral. WESTPAC deployment exercises were developing requirements for CONUS numbers—more than were routinely deployed. SEALS were written into PACOM Special Operations Annexes to War Plans. The guild was returning to the lilly. The post-war understandable lethargy was slowly abating. Officers were getting promoted. Staffs were jousting for SpecWar assignments from BUPERS; the demand was exceeding the supply. In SEAL Team ONE we were enthused by the renewed attention. "Steady as you go" was our order of the day. Officers started assignments to numbered fleets—Sixth and Seventh Fleets (the ARGs never lost their lieutenant commander SEAL/UDT staff slots). People were coming of age for staff college attendance. Slowly, billets were forming on larger staffs—CNO and JCS. The true dawn would not occur until mid-eighties, notably with Irish Flynn's selection. What we could do at the team level was perform in fleet and joint exercises and gain recognition. From our standpoint, all we needed is not to suffer the neglect of the mid-sixties, that is, no resources for an outboard engine. With our groups in place with CNO/OPNAV coverage, we were able to compete for service funding. Our OPNAV sponsor was the Surface Warfare Directorate—anything that floated except carriers and submarines. Competing for funds (resources) was a "labor union" dogfight between aviators, who needed to pay for carriers and aircraft; submariners, who had nuclear reactors to fund; and ship-driving "black shoes" who steamed cruisers, destroyers, logistics ships, and amphibious landing ships. Ours was a hard sell among the barnacle-crusted "salts" of the "E ring." Happily, I was still a lieutenant commander with a team to feed. My big budget battles would have to wait until 1979. In the meantime, I relinquished command of SEAL Team ONE to Lieutenant Commander Grant Telfer.

I had orders to report to the Defense Attaché School before deploying to Cambodia as Naval Attache'. Included therewith were six weeks of French language refresher at the State Language School in Roslyn, Virginia. Attaché School was over in Anacostia, Maryland. June, July, and August were spent in D.C. That completed I had a couple of weeks leave and attended that Masters' Swimming Championship mentioned before. It's always ticked me how Pelloux know I was coming back. French intelligence? I did once phone him at the *Sportif* pool: "*Docteur Pelloux, Docteur Pelloux (tinkle, tinkle bel) . . . Qui, c'est moi . . .*" Yuk, yuk.

On to Phom Penh to relieve Lieutenant Commander Dick Marcinko, who did a wonderful job with the Khmer Navy. His would be tough shoes to fill. Dick is what I term a "biological leader." Although some would chafe with his deliberate drive, his ability to endear himself with his troops—and notably the Khmer sailor—was magnificent.

But what'd I learn from his command? Probably more than four years at the Naval Academy could possibly implant. Primarily, listen to the troops, starting especially with the chiefs; never leave a CPO out of the decision loop. I should have learned that with my first assignment. First of all, do not try or attempt to do the chief's job, that is, don't micromanage. Any "good idea" needs the chief's support, that's a good place to start. Period.

SEAL Team requalifying for military freefall training outside San Diego.
SEAL Team trainees get this before graduation today. Every jump
is a "requal leap!" Here I am re-enlisting another sailor. At the time,
1972, the gear was pick-up stuff: ski cloves, Bell motorcycle helmet,
French paraboots, crossbow parachute with back-mounted reserver—all
personally owned. It's better today!

My chain of command: Command Master Chief-Senior Chief Claude
Willis presents me with a SEAL Team plaque. A decorated SEAL
operator in Vietnam, Senior Chief Willis was indispensable to command
policies. (My father is in the background with his camera, seeking a shot.
He was a shutterbug!)

CHAPTER 10

MY STATE DEPARTMENT TOUR AND FOLLOW-ON

In 1974 the United States was supporting the Khmer Republic (Cambodia) against the Communist, China-supported *Khmer Rouge* ("Red Khmer"). The strategic bombing had been stopped that summer, but the advisory effort labored on. Following Attaché School and French language refresher, I alighted in the capital city late September. I was ready to snap photos from my armpit—a skill taught at Attaché School, unnecessary in Cambodia. I was the numerical relief for Lieutenant Commander Dick Marcinko, who was in receipt of orders to command SEAL Team TWO. Our turnover was a week of "hail and farewell" parties. We had two "bosses," Ambassador John Gunther Dean, a World War II refugee from NAZI Germany, headed up the embassy "country team"; the other organization was the Military Equipment Delivery Team, Cambodia [MEDTC (Med-Tech)] and was commanded by Brigadier General William Palmer, USA.

My immediate superior was Army Colonel L.B. Martin, USA, an Armor Officer in "real life"—the era slang seeping in. The Naval Attaché's principle job was to liaise with the Cambodian Navy. This required daily chitchats with their chief of Naval Operations Rear Admiral, Vong Sarendy, a charismatic guy who was selfless in looking after his Navy. I won't delve into accusations rife in the embassy and MEDTC about the corruption inside other *Khmer* services. Accusations against Vietnam leadership was everywhere acknowledged and probably went back years. Little has been written about Cambodian corruption.

I was assigned a house (not "villa") two miles from the embassy. The job was with a car and driver (more later). A young family was assigned to cook and clean—So Tan (hard "a", not "tan"), his wife, and young child; later, his brother's family moved in (at my expense). So Tan was a pretty good cook. I would hit the morning brief on a cup of coffee and return around eight for some breakfast. I had some personal effects accompany me, not a house full. I would host occasional receptions for the staff and other (limited) foreign attachés—cocktails and hors d'oeuvres, nothing late. These pretty much petered out as 1975 wore on. Nobody wants to be sipping gin during a mortar attack! And the embassy wives were relocated to Bangkok. The job got more pressure as time wore on. There was no way FANK could stem the *Khmer Rouge* tide. Convoys reduced transits until finally they were cancelled when the ammo barge was captured—tugboat sank. Airlift increased and were earlier used to resupply Army outposts. On a personal note, that first month in Cambodia, I came down with a strain of flu and dysentery. I found myself air-evacuated to Thailand at the hospital clinic at U-Ta-Pow. I felt near death.

With a saline infusion and antibiotics, I pulled through; lost twenty pounds and I was in great swimming shape at 185. I slouched into my first staff morning meeting a size under the clothes I arrived in. I was translucent, barely cast a shadow. Recovery took a month, and the attaché pace never slowed.

In addition to becoming close with Sarendy, I made twice daily—sometimes all day long, and nights—visits to the Navy operations center. Khmer Navy Commander Kieu Sampan was the operations officer. His office ran all the Mekong River operations and coordinated defense for Mekong River Convoys, which were scheduled by the embassy with MACV. Cambodia air, marine, and naval forces met the convoy at 0700 at the Vietnam-Cambodian border. The trick was to get the supply ship to Phnom Penh before sunset. These convoys involved the Naval Attaché as a member of the Tri-Partite Committee consisting of representatives from Vietnam, Cambodia, and the U.S. These meetings were held quarterly in Saigon at Navy headquarters. Sarendy and the Vietnamese Navy Operations officer were classmates from the French Naval Academy and got along well. My third attendance at this meeting was mid-March 1975, a month before the two countries collapsed. Saigon was bustling—brass shining, no diesel fumes, streets clean, bustling stores—no indication that the end was about to erupt in the north. We (CIA, State, Defense) hadn't a clue! Except PACOM and the Seventh Fleet were drafting "Eagle Pull," an extraction operation to evacuate embassy personnel and selective Cambodians. Two Marine Corps colonels came to Phnom Penh to begin the study for an Operation Order. This was early March.

Daily briefings were held with the Ambassador at 0800 and 1700. At these "dumps" we were updated on *Khmer Rouge* movements and Army activity to defend, Intel "captures," and forthcoming delivery schedules. The British and Australian ambassadors often attended, not regularly but frequently. Following the morning dump, usually half hour, I was able to head over to Navy HQ around 0900. I would loiter there for about two hours, including occasional coffee with Sarendy. We would review upcoming operations and results of overnight missions. Too often, his boats would take hits from the river banks. On one particular spectacular *Khmer Rouge* ambush on a barge convoy northeast of Phnom Penh, Ambassador Dean was livid. His anger was misplaced, considering a war was ongoing. Sarendy was in the middle of an initiative the ambassador would need to approve. It fell to me to deliver the bad news. I had to make a cover story for embassy non-concurrence, to wit: some prattle excuse that the lost equipment would need Navy "issue resources" to replace. I had no doubt he could see right through my alibi. Ah, diplomacy . . . we remained friends. Time for fun.

Before 1975 there was time for some fun. Throughout my tour I was able to swim in the Circle Sportif Phnom Penh pool, with an occasional tennis venture—around noon, the hottest time of the day. Swimming was more comfortable. There were several decent French restaurants in Phnom Penh. Once, my French doctor pal from Saigon, selling pharmaceuticals on the side, came to PP; another old Saigon acquaintance was housed there, and we raced through the fall rain downfall and arrived for dinner completely drenched. Happy was I with my State Department French language refresher course. It has been my foreign language experience with French, German, and Spanish that one needs full emersion for four months before the light comes on. I later used my Berlitz German in Stuttgart and Spanish during ship liberty in Spain. Not easy.

On good days we would go out onto the Mekong to test out maintenance on riverine craft. Often, we would fly down to Neuk

Loung, the halfway town to Vietnam. When Mekong Convoys were steaming, we would fly them overhead—starting at the border and generally making Phnom Penh before sunset. Before 1975 these were routine transits, rarely taking fire. All would change on New Year's Day 1975 when *Khmer Rouge* forces throughout the country attacked its Republic forces.

The "last act" of the Khmer Republic opened New Year's Eve. The Embassy was hosting a celebratory New Year's party. Not many of us stayed around for midnight given the 0730 requirement to brief. But the dawn brought calamitous news: the *Khmer Rouge* had staged attacks throughout the country and specially along the entire length of the Cambodian Mekong River. The marine base at Neuk Loung was completely sacked. There was excited reaction throughout the embassy and MEDTC with emergency powwows. FLASH messages were sent to CINCPAC, State Department, CIA, and the Defense Intelligence Agency. All the staffing "stovepipes" were lit up. Of course, no recourse was available—much like today's posture in Iraq. We didn't realize it but Khmer Republic days were numbered. Marshall Lon Nol and the Joint Staff were frozen. The days of partying with "Hennessey and soda" were over. It was a disaster. Word from Hawaii was to increase protection for the Mekong Convoys which provided food and ammunition to Phnom Penh. Soon, within a month, refugees began crowding the outskirts of the city. Our embassy briefings continued with news of the spreading "red ink blot" extinguishing government outposts one after the other. The noose tightened.

Three days into January, I suggested to Colonel Martin that we needed, or MEDTC needed, to get to Neuk Loung to inventory how much was lost. General Palmer agreed, and so two of us hopped on an Air America chopper to get down river and count heads. When we arrived, we discovered the commander had retired to his bed and was not seen since the attack. When we rousted him from his quarters, he hadn't shaved; he allowed he would shave when *Khmer Rouge* were off the river! (What was this, Stanley Cup playoffs?)

We diligently spent several hours counting lost rifles and people. The toll was staggering, and the U.S. had to replace it; but where would the manpower come from? At this moment, the Khmer Navy's fledging Marine unit ceased to be a force of any impact. There was no leadership fit to regenerate the capability. The army and air corps were barely hanging on. Vong Sarendy's riverine troops had plenty of PBRs—as well as some swift boats at Sihanoukville on the coast, but they were miles away from the Mekong. On our way back home, we could hear the snap of rounds passing our helicopter. "C'mon, guys, 1500 feet ain't hacking it in a Huey!"

The convoys became the lifeblood of Phnom Penh. I continued to fly them. On one occasion we were delayed to Neuk Loung while the civilian crews balked at continuing to run the gauntlet without a pay increase. Sarendy wanted to shoot some of them—Philippines. Ambassador Dean didn't take the news well, either. Well, none of us did. An Army Attaché suggested that "money talks." Something had to be done to safeguard the merchant ships. PACOM Admiral Noel Gayler came to Phnom Penh looking for answers. Consensus was to construct wire mesh over the pilot houses of the transports, the idea being they would activate a B-40 rocket round before it struck the ship. Construction would begin at Vung Tau, Vietnam. About a half dozen were built.

I cannot recall a single one defeating a B-40; none were fired— and I had flown every convoy. I do, however, recall a barge-and ocean-going tugboat hitting a command detonated mine; the tug sank in sixty seconds. (These, too, were modified with cushioning in the pilot houses.) At some time we had Khmer Air Force choppers provide coverage—spotty as it was. Their fixed win planes make bombing passes as suspected ambush sites. At dusk the choppers would let loose a hail of .50 caliber rounds, which in the lower light tracers could be easily identified falling on targets. But none were qualified for night ops so they had to be back before sunset. The proverbial tealeaves were not falling on a democratic outcome.

Our daily life was dwindling down to desperation. FANK (Khmer Army Forces) outposts were falling daily without relief. The Mekong was slowly being choked off. A Congressional delegation was received around mid-March, mostly with preconceived notions of cutting funding. Which happened. It was useless to brief them, and the ambassador gave it his best shot—a thankless task! Their minds were made up. Accusations over who lost the countries continue to this day.

All the while the *Khmer Rouge* noose was tightening on Phnom Penh. By the middle of March (1975) Communist troops had slithered into the eastern bank of the Mekong opposite Phnom Penh and the Navy Base at Churry Changwar, a short bridge trip across a Mekong tributary. (French Navy instructors were still holding classes!) Mortar rounds were starting to land downtown. One attack hit the Central Market, killing several civilians. Occasionally, a blast could be heard at the embassy.

On one occasion the Navy wanted to coordinate an amphibious operation on a suspected *Khmer Rouge* assembly on the lower Mekong western bank. Troops would be disgorged onto the bank supported by PBRs and helicopter gunships. All well and good. I mustered at the air base with Admiral Serendy and an Army Major General who was accompanied by several batmen with picnic baskets stuffed with food, beer, and scotch. Brigadier General Ea

Chung would pilot "Air Force ONE," a C-47 with seats, as airborne command post—yuk, yuk. Before wheels were up, the Army guy was asleep. Sarendy and I chortled. It took thirty minutes to arrive over "Green Beach" at 8000 feet altitude—fairly safe from AK-47 rounds or B-40 rockets. The approaching LCU looked like it was loaded with ants; I asked Ea Chung to drop down to 3000 feet—settling for 4500. Zzzzzz . . . from the rear of the plane—the Army artillery guy, a snoring mouth breather. But before long it was time for lunch—okay, a ham sandwich and 7-UP. The LCM amphibious craft had departed Phnom Penh several hours before. The craft were twenty-five yards off shore when the *Khmer Rouge* opened fire. In spite of government chopper strafing runs, the defensive fire was not suppressed. The craft withdrew—a sad day for democracy. Ah shucks. The artillery "expert" went back to sleep.

As a rule, supposedly backed by law, attachés were not supposed to expose themselves to enemy fire. We were not "advisors." Our portfolio was to review and report. Well, we argued, one had to get close enough to review and find out what was happening. We weren't advising, we were suggesting. And the information MEDTC needed could only come with proximity. One of the MEDTC officers was Marine Corps Lieutenant Colonel John Hopkins, 1956 Naval Academy graduate and captain of the 1955 Navy football team. Great guy, good officer, great sense of humor. He spent as much time in the Navy's HQ as I did. Much later, when he was a retiring Major General, I flew up to Twenty-Nine Palms for the ceremony. Lieutenant General Bill Keyes, a Classmate of mine from Marine Corps Command and Staff College and National War College, was also there. I was the sole naval officer at the ceremony. A few years later I attended Hopkins' funeral at the Marine Corps Base, Cape Pendleton.

Things were getting dicey in Phnom Penh. Mekong Convoys had halted. Electrical interruption was daily; local generators noisily kept lights and air conditioning on. Mortar bodies were an everyday occurrence. Sunday morning, April 13, around nine, I got a cellphone call from Colonel Martin. He told me to pack out and be at Pochentong Airport in three hours for a C-130 evac to Thailand. "So Tan, get truck!" Massive effort to box stuff and get to the airport. All happened with alacrity and sadness. I hugged So Tan and gave him the Cambodian money I had and boarded the "Hercules" for the forty-minute flight to Thailand's U Ta Pow Air Base. On arrival, I checked my baggage and headed to Pattaya Beach to find a hotel. That evening, I went to Dolf Rick's restaurant for dinner, then made my way via bus to Bangkok and the U.S. Embassy, which Navy Attaché was waiting with reservation in a downtown hotel, coopted as a Bachelor Quarters.

The Air Attaché, Air Force Colonel Doug Royston (Naval Academy Class of 1957), had also been separately evacuated. The Army Defense Attachés were retained; Navy and Air Corps operations had essentially stalled. The Embassy Country Team remained in Phnom Penh for a week when Eagle Pull was executed; everyone was flown out by Marine helicopters to Seventh Fleet ships to be later united in Bangkok. The Cambodian team would be in Bangkok for a month. The Khmer Republic remained in office another week before the Khmer Rouge marched into town to accept surrender. Some hours before that I had been in phone contact with the Navy staff; they begged for relief. They, as with the Joint Staff, were stripped naked and murdered. The same day, every civilian, including hospital sick and infirm, were herded out of town into the country to undergo four years of concentration camp genocide. (A book to read is *Cambodge annee zero*, by Francois Ponchaud (Julliard, Paris, 1977—in French.)

Now, a political comment: not a single left-winger complained about the genocide. It turned out later to be the North Vietnamese Army (NVA) that booted Pol Pot and his thugs out. In fact, one of the ring leaders was—"is," still in trial—Khieu Sampan, the *Khmer Rouge* Operations Officer. (Not a peep when African genocide occurred years later during the Clinton Administration.)

In company with Ambassador Dean, several attachés visited the refugee camp; happy I was to see my driver, Pak Ban—as in Asia, family name is first—and his family. Later they were transferred to Alexandria where I caught up with them. I helped with housing and stayed in touch right up to 2009 when both Ban and his wife passed away. The kids all got to college, speak fluent English, and have made lives for themselves.

On one occasion, still in Thailand, we were in the embassy plan enroute U-Ta-Pow airport. Fifteen minutes out we were advised by approach control to loiter a mile out at 3000 feet. Turns out a squadron Vietnamese Air Force fighter planes were coming, they're crammed with families fleeing the NVA closing on Saigon. Stacked above us were a couple of C-141 planes and there may have been more! The Viets landed and immediately formed up to march off the field. Thai airmen ran out to the planes and painted out the Vietnamese markings. After the half hour hullabaloo, we landed. What a scene. It was the weekend before the fall of Saigon. We were going to Pattaya Beach for the weekend. What a welcome!

That last week of April 1975 was momentous as we observed from a sideline the fall of South Vietnam. At our de facto BOQ American Embassy staffers and others crowded into the bar. There was an overall sentiment of sorrow, which we Phnom Penh evictees could relate to. So ended our multi-year relationship with the fledging democracy—from aiding France since the end of World War II to April 29, 1975. We lent support to the first Vietnamese War, France versus the *Viet Minh,* then we took over after Dien Bien Phu (1954)—for two decades and 58,000 names on the Wall in Washington. And the question persist: where'd we go wrong? Which discussion might bring us closer to home in 2015?

What'd I learn in Attaché School, Language School refresher, in an embassy community, in Cambodia writ large? DIA Attaché School imparted an appreciation for "intelligence," that little bits of information can be singular blocks of a larger façade. Opening that proverbial door is the skill of analysis. We attachés worked closely with the embassy station chief and other nondescript covered agents. Intelligence is a competitive engagement, jealously protected. I had no desire to complete. Admiral Sarendy had a soft spot for one female agent, and she played her cards diplomatically. I hid nothing from her from my standpoint. The agency had people all over the place, but I am not certain where. Next, I started learning the old adage about catching more flies with honey was true. (I cemented this fact later in the Pentagon working with GS employees.)

Language refresher—six hours a day with memorization homework—left me with headaches. I clearly learned that total emersion was required to get any competency in French. They cut off half the words in speech. To sound a final consonant required an "e" or "-tion" on the end of a noun; adjectives had to agree in gender and case (masculine/feminine, possessive, objective); gender drives verbs, nouns, adjectives, and adverbs.

All I knew about Cambodia was what I had read in the Army Country Guide. I had met a Cambodian girl in Saigon three years before, her father was a *Khmer Crum* from the Vietnamese Delta and a senator in the Vietnamese government. She was much darker than the local Viets, who were lighter. And when my clock started in Phnom Penh, it took me thirty days to be able to see the beauty of the Khmer race!

This chapter title has "follow-on" in it, so by way of a "post script" a few lines. After my return home—and blame for losing the country burned out—I was ready to continue my service in August 1975 at the Marine Corps Command and Staff College in Quantico, Virginia. This was an opportunity to rub shoulders with officers from all services and some foreign students. We had a Canadian Lieutenant Commander in our section, which was led by Lieutenant Colonel Festa, who as a platoon commander in Vietnam had been the unit in which Vietnam historian Bernard Fall was killed by a mine explosion. Fall had written *La Rue sans Joie* and *Hell in a Very Small Place.* C&S offered instruction on corps policy and a general look at national security. Guest speakers included Ambassador Henry Kissinger and CIA Chief Admiral Stansfield Turner, among others. It was a fun nine months during which I learned to be appreciative of joint opinions. And we all gained a greater appreciation for the Marine Corps—specially, for example, the corps' argument for close support aircraft pilots with Marine uniforms.

ATTACHE/STATE DEPARTMENT TOUR

The Defense Intelligence Agency Attaché School (six months) taught prospective attachés to love their cameras, and to report on everything. In post-1973 Cambodia and Vietnam, we were prohibited from going into the field in combat. Huh? Subject to rocket attack in Phnom Penh the "FEBA" was across the street. And weren't supposed to "advise" either. But discussing operational options was always a dinner table delicacy. I flew every Mekong River Convoy for seven months. I flew in "Air Force ONE" on riverine operations—reporting on progress.

In country identification papers: "Republique Khmere
Carte d'Identite dimplomatique."

Chief of Cambodian Naval Operations Commodore, Vong Sarendy:
"To my dear George, My most Sincere and affectual friendship." He was
about forty-five and well-respected on both sides. Graduate of the French
Naval Academy, his classmate was operations officer in the Vietnamese
Navy; they coordinated on Mekong Convoy security. I sat on the Convoy
Tri-Partite Committee that met every quarter in Saigon to plan and
organize the effort.

Chapter 11

INSHORE UNDERSEA WARFARE GROUP ONE

Here is the tale of one of my most enjoyable tours: leading the West Coast group called U.S. Naval Inshore Undersea Warfare Group ONE. The "undersea" element came from running marine mammals and underwater, offshore sonar arrays. Doesn't sound thrilling, but it turned out to be one of the most gratifying assignments I ever had. And 99 percent of the assigned enlisted sailors would look back in agreement—including all the women we had assigned. Was it challenging? The technology, sure; the people, nope . . . except one early adventure into "SEAL Team" physical training regimen. The Teams had always had what were termed "Monster Mashers," full-team Friday exercise competitions—running, boat paddling, swimming, PT (push-ups, chinning, etc.). The women were embarrassed having to dress out in Speedo racing suits. But, whoa . . . in my enthusiasm I'm getting way ahead of myself, jumping into the havoc without displaying the "Block Diagram" of the chain of command.

1976 was very much still in a "Post-Vietnam" shell. The Naval Special Warfare community was still holding on to its structure. In this circumstance, it welcomed any "flesh" to the skeleton. The disparate make-up of IUWGs was an example of this; Marine Mammal Program—dolphins and sea lions, and sensors, off-shore acoustic sensors. Half the command were SEALS running the mammals; a quarter oriented on the Ho Chi Minh Trail; a quarter looking for Soviet submarines off San Diego. It was also home to a significant of reservists—with built-in reserve headaches. The mammal program migrated to Naval Special Warfare because of base closing in Long Beach. EOD ran the program up there; the program came to Naval Special Warfare almost by default—well, totally by default. Coronado SEALs were selected to shepherd the sea lions and dolphins. Our human "SEALs" loved the program. Sea lions recovered rocket casings, dolphins guarded bridges and underwater approaches from swimmers. The land and sea sensors were both technical orientation requiring electronics techs and communicators. What could be seen as a boring assignment? Not on your life. To work exercises, we had to receive reservists and plan the beachfront approaches with acoustic sensors. In the "outback," sensors were stashed around outposts. The mammals protected the Coronado Bay Bridge and the amphib base. Everybody had a mission.

Now, back to Monster Mashes. With half the Group SEALs, the remainder could not possibly compete—if the SEALs competed as a distinct department. Needed to scatter the wealth, so we set up "Blue and Gold Teams" with half the SEALs on each and the other people assorted equitably. The women accepted the tank suits and a mutiny was avoided. Our Mashes were held once a quarter. Starting at 1000 they consisted of the CISM obstacle course, a beach run, and pool competition of several overturned IBS (Inflatable Rubber Boats) facing each other in the base fifty-meter pool—all followed by a hamburger and bean cookout in the command compound. End-of-games was around 1300 and everyone set off on the weekend. Lots of fun and good cheer—one time it made *Navy Times* with a photo of one lady negotiating the O-Course.

My real adventure was to start when another SEAL, John Sandoz, mused that the NDW groups needed better communications. Hmmm. There's an idea out of the "Mind of Minolta!" Again, now 1977, Navy hadn't spent a nickel on land sensors since observation of the Ho Chi Minh trail had been shut down following the Paris Peace Accords. And none was forthcoming. What if we addressed ourselves to communicating? My "Comm/ET" experience to this point included communications officer in Halsey Powell and operations officer in Strong plus sundry mobile Tacticals Ops Center (TOC) set-up in UDT and SEAL Teams. This was my first experience looking at NSW group tactical communications requirements, an organic capability without reliance on a supporting activity or service (like "over-the-counter" message delivery). Group needed UHF tactical voice for platoons, VHF for vehicles, HF for long haul, and SatCom. I was reminded of our Christmas Island deployment rigging a "long wire" (HF) from our masthead to stern for comms with Hawaii. I was painfully aware, too, that Group ONE, Captain John O'Drain, while approving of the effort, had no money to buy radios. We were a prime example of an "unfunded requirement." POM it—see it three years out. Not good enough, but happily for us, "Big Navy" was shedding ships and with them their radios. Why not corner a close-out vessel and purloin their radios—and crypto systems. Certain radios and all cryptology elements were registered. Tokens, so we would require

Naval Communications Command authorization (and responsible security agencies). Long story short—we got all required up checks; now the drill was to notify the ships identified and pick up gear.

The radiomen and electronics technicians mounted in our trucks and headed north to Long Beach to gather gear. The Pacific Fleet ships in San Diego were "free five zones" for our reapers. Suffice it to say, we got all we could use. During the gathering, other techs dismantled the ground sensor gear from the walls of our lead-lined Battle Area Surveillance System (BASS) vans. In fact, these were so well-constructed when the Naval Security Agency official tested our security he could not register a ray of escaping electronic communications leakage. We were "cleared in hot" to go on fleet exercises with the title "Naval Special Warfare Mobile Comm Team (MCT)." Years later, when I acceded to command NSW ONE, I was able to reap the rewards of my OPNAV work with getting gear. Since I had departed IUWG-1 (1978) during the interval funding was identified and state-of-the-art vans developed. When I accepted Group, we had two CE (Command and Control Communications) vans. I deployed one to Korea for Operation "Foal Eagle," for us centered at Korean Navy Base Chinhae. As Group Commander, I could communicate worldwide, all crypto secure. We even set up a twenty-five yard long wire for high frequency. My Korean Navy counterpart was impressed; frankly, so was I. We had a Tactical Ops Center alongside and were able to monitor platoon chatter from the field.

During the remainder of my time at IUWG-1 and later, the MCT was manned by our people. Ownership, always with the Group, was later absorbed in staff manning documents. The positions are full permanent billets with a Special Duty Lieutenant Commander Officer in Charge. In the nineties, during surveys for a photo-anthology, I learned that the MCT today deploys with upwards of fifty tons of comm gear and fifteen people! I will let the reader conclude if this is impressive. I was.

I migrated from IUWG-1 to the National War College; a year later I was in the Naval Special Warfare Sponsor's Directorate within OP-37, led by former submariner Real Admiral Harry Schrader (RIP). A pugnacious bulldog, I loved the guy. There was no mistaking his desires, no fear of a misplaced "Aye, aye, Sir." Your ass was in your own hands! I remember one day, early in my tour, the Admiral's secretary phone me. "The Admiral needs a quick blurb on riverine warfare!" Yikes! Quick, where in the stack did I remember a pitch on riverine warfare. Civil War: history all laid out—get crackin'. Made it with five minutes to spare as the boss started trekking down the passageway to Vice Admiral Walters's (OP-03) office. Whew! Live another day. I knew that all along. Well, I wasn't going to forget it.

One item of staffing interest: acceptability of retaining SEALs in charge of the Marine Mammal Program. Land sensors had long since evaporated from funding documents—read approval. Next, findings mines: SEALs will find them and blow them up, obviating the possibility of identifying origin or technology. We had enjoyed our post-Vietnam hiatus; time running around in t-shirts and flip-flops, on the southeast of the base, outta sight of the flagpole. Things were tightening up further East—way beyond El Cajon or Little Creek. Direct Action SEAL platoons had departed Saigon in December 1971. Eight years later, it was time to re-evaluate doctrine and capabilities. I wrote a point paper recommending shifting the entire Marine Mammal Program to the Explosive Ordnance Disposal (EOD) community. With all the interim "chopping," fleet approval, etc.; it was approved. The interlude was embraced by Naval Special Warfare as a respite and "filler" to protect the Group existence. It's difficult figuring where to insert the quotation marks. Looking back,

CNO Zumwalt's memorandum to solidify the Groups went far to endanger the community. But insecurity feeds paranoia, which was learned over many years. Padding with IUWGs was another sandbag on the dike against the river's rising. By the time we relinquished IUWGs, a new era was closing in.

July 1978, I was in receipt of orders to the National War College, Class of 1979. War College was strategic reading, lectures, case studies, class discussions, time with families ... and more reading. Five hundred pages a night wasn't unusual. It would have been "unusual" had I read much of them. What counted was class participation. It was, all in all, an enjoyable nine months, couple of decent trips, one of which was to New York and visits to business and Wall Street—and good NYC chow. (I had some friends there, too, which was nice.) We stayed at a mid-town Marriott, chockablock with creature comforts. Busses to various briefings. New York is bustling—a "Number One" target we later learned in 1993 and 9/11. War College graduated in June 1979. I reported into Navy Staff, Naval Operations (OPNAV), Surface Warfare Directorate (OP-03), specifically, the aforementioned OP-37 with the Amphibious Warfare Division (OP-474). An interesting and challenging period awaited me.

What'd I learn from IUWG? Follow your instincts. I felt—knew—NSW didn't know communications from my shipboard experience I felt certain we had a capability gap to fill. The engineers at NAVELEX and the detachment at Saint Inigoes, MD, concurred. They did the lion's share of the development, which came well after I had departed. But what I threw stuck to the wall. Nowhere in this Navy can you do it all yourself. But a viable project will attract capable people, which is what happened with the C3 Van project. Our home-built "erector set" caught the imagination of the people in the right engineering circles. It was done.

IUWG C3 VAN TEAM

Inshore Undersea Warfare Group ONE, Mobile Communications Team
(MCT), 1977 and ongoing. Staffed with electronics technicians and
radiomen, we revamped our Army Battle Area Surveillance Systems
(BASS) vans into command and control communications vans affording
an organic C3 communications Capability to the Naval Special Warfare
Group(s). We deployed to Korea (1987), and I relied on it during
DESERT STORM.

CHAPTER 12

THE PENTAGON INTERLUDE

After eighteen years of line assignments—destroyers, Naval Special Warfare, Service Schools (UDT Replacement Training, Army Basic and Freefall Parachute, Destroyer Department Head, Defense Attaché and two War Colleges)—I held orders to the Pentagon Navy Staff (OPNAV) in the Surface Warfare Directorate, OP-03. The Pentagon "E" Ring encompasses the offices of the Service Chiefs. The mission Specific Navy specialties (Directorates) are three-star (Vice Admiral) positions. Subordinate warfare breakdowns are headed up by more junior flag officers. I was detailed tow OP-37, responsible for Amphibious and Mine Warfare and specialties of Explosive Ordnance Disposal (EOD) and Naval Special Warfare (SEAL, UDT, and Special Boats). I went to the Naval Special Warfare sub-division headed by one of our SEAL Commanders, Jim Barnes, a former Commanding Officer of SEAL Team ONE.

In 1979 officers wore civilian clothes to work. Uniforms were worn on Wednesdays. Pentagon duty is viewed with fear by many. Why should officers interrupt sea duty and sparse shore assignments close to the waterfront to learn the budget system. I can complain about money and the lack thereof from team experience discussed earlier about not getting two outboard engines—which forced a five-mile ocean paddle during a 1966 insertion. By July 1979 we were doing moderately better—recalling my success with communications in Inshore Undersea Warfare Group ONE . . . and about which more to come.

Culture Shock

A major social adjustment in the Pentagon was, and remains, the encounter with career civilians. This plain-clothed cohort has seen a thousand guys like me from the fleet and field leaping into their *pukkas* demanding "goods and services" for the units they left behind. Whew! Another firebrand wanting resources NOW! "Mind your manners" is the best advice I can offer, and I came by it surprisingly gently. Short story—the units they left behind. At that time we had the *Stinger* precursor anti-air manpack missile, *Redeye,* in the ammo locker that required periodic maintenance tests, etc. Jim Barnes told me to slip over to OP-411, the Navy bullet counting desk, and inquire about servicing (we had no money!). I walked from our 4ᵗʰ ring—4D537 (will never forget the address)—to "3-C something." I slipped in as unceremoniously as possible in my four-piece suit and introduced myself to retired Navy Commander Jack Jester and his assistant, Ms. Lois Goldberg. I explained in plaintive terms our problem and asked for maintenance recommendations—nothing broken but you want your missile to work. (By the way, *Redeye* was a "revenge" weapon whose heat-seeking radar required a shot as an attacking aircraft was outbound for an exhaust presentation; *Stinger* accepts a 360-degree presentation—hopefully before you get smoked!) Jack asked how many; I replied sixty. Jack picked up the phone and called Ms. Wanda Justice at Naval Material Command in Crystal City (the go-between of OPNAV and Navy Systems Commands, later decommissioned) and asked if she could pick up the SEAL account. (Years later, Ms. Justice came West to work for me at Naval Special Warfare Command.) "Mission accomplished," I was able to report to Barnes. The lesson for me at my first month in OPNAV was, "You catch more flies with honey." In truth, too, I became a frequent visitor to "411" for coffee with Lois, who forgot more about ammunition accounting than I can relate—training ammo, war reserves, operational ammo, Reserve allocations, surface-air-submarine accounts, and of course SEAL Team small arms. A myth has it that in the first year of commissioning (1981) SEAL Team SIX fired more .45 caliber rounds than the entire Marine Corps—Lois and Jack to account for those rounds.

Moving Up the Staircase

I spent one year I OP-372. Barnes was relieved in summer '80 by Commander Maynard Weyers. I got shuffled upstairs to the fifth floor newly established Directorate of Naval Warfare (OP-095), the brainchild of CNO Tom Hayward. My specific office code was OP-954; Strike Warfare, responsible for Air, Amphibs, and Surface task organizations. The "095" Directorate was charged with finding commonalities between engineering sub-systems and cross-mission sets—carrier aviation, submarines, amphibious, and surface strike forces. I found myself writing a memo a day conjuring up potential missions for SEALs and Frogmen. For example, 1980 was a year of rampant turmoil in the Persian Gulf. I thought we might need some hydrographic Intel about the surrounding coastlines—today's littoral regions of such interest we build ships for it. My idea was to send a SEAL to a local embassy, pick a potential landing beach, wade out and record the depth, bottom contour, sand consistency, natural obstacles. No takers, but a decade later (1990) we were in the Persian Gulf with no hydrographic charts.

Program Development

Naval Special Warfare needed modern communications—command and control suites for Groups and tactical communications for SEAL Team maneuver elements—above and beyond PR-9 briquettes whose squelch button blanked out all comms. In 1977 I was at Inshore Undersea Warfare Group ONE. Vietnam-era land surveillance gear was no longer in use or anticipated. We took that gear off the walls of our Army Battle Area Surveillance System (BASS) vans were completely lead lined so we're "silent" electronically—no spurious signal leaks. The idea was to afford Group staffs an organic command and control communications capability. We assembled one in Coronado with command funds and radios from retiring Fleet ships. We employed the first one in local Southern California Fleet exercises and deployed it to Korea for Exercise Foal Eagle, operating out of Chin Hae Navy Base in southern South Korea. An ultimate result of the C3 comm vans was to establish Mobile Comm Teams (MCT) at each Naval Special Warfare Group staffed with permanent duty radiomen and electronics technicians. Ultimately, working from OP-054 we were able to get Commander Naval Telecommunications Command (COMNAVTELCOM) to formalize an omnibus Naval Special Warfare Communications Plan and fund new C3 vans for the two Groups. Great assistance came from the NAVELEX (Naval Electronics System Integration Command) in Salisbury, southeastern Maryland. (Later I sat on a BRAC Board with Maryland's Senator Paul Sarbanes and Congressman Stenny Hoyer to defend keeping the NAVELEX of the Chopping block. One main reason: the airwaves down range in Salisbury are relatively clear of multiple television, radio, and airport communications.)

Civilian clothes in the Pentagon affordability the ability to sit with action officers without "front office" curiosity. As a Commander "Action Officer" I could slink around without question and deal with all ranks on issues. When Reagan put us all back in uniform and I made Captain, I couldn't go low profile into staff stalls with impunity without energizing front office curiosity. "What's that strange '06' doing with my people?" And as soon as you pin on "Captain" stripes no one wants to talk with you! Running around the halls as an "05" three striper one had "Go For" status—everybody assumes you're on a fact-gathering mission, so a smile and a little schmoozing grease goes far . . . part of that "honey" lesson.

The most compelling and influential action I initiated while in OP-954 was to develop a Naval Special Warfare Master Plan (NSWMP) (1981). When I announced to the Naval Special Warfare Groups all I heard back was, "daunting, can't be done, nobody has access . . . etc." I submitted my proposal up the chain; meanwhile, I was called to brief Vice Admiral McKee, OP-095, on a frigid fall Saturday morning. I had my NAVSEA viewgraph pitch well rehearsed. The audience included his aide, a friend, Commander Bob Natter, and an unknown staff Captain. At brief's end I alluded to my desire to compose a Naval Special Warfare Master Plan laying out SEAL Team requirements. "Wish list," some suggested. The idea was to illuminate Naval Special Warfare goals and objectives. For example, one goal was mobility—subsumed "objectives highlighted submarines, surface support shipping, team organic boats (ZODIACs), and other combatant craft maintained by the (then named) Coastal-Riverine Squadrons. Other objectives under assorted goals are small arms, medical, diving, MILCON. McKee approved the effort and allocated $65,000. It might do well to recall that OP-095, McKee, was the OPNAV "master plan" Guru at the time sponsoring such exposes on Anti-Submarine Warfare, Mine Warfare, Electronics Warfare. The glimmer for a SEAL master plan had abiding suggestion. The plan formation was approved. The Columbia research writer and I started out the effort, which took about six months visits to each group and collaboration with other OPNAV codes. The finished draft, NSWMP (PLAN), had to pass through reviews of all the "E" Ring Barons. Took half a year. In the meantime, I was ordered, again, back downstairs to 4D537 to start my fourth year in the "puzzle palace."

Most career officers are dedicated to a specific branch or warfighting community. One needs to achieve in a special in order to survive the next selection board for rank progression. An officer's reputation gets known as he or she advances. Stopping in mid-career to learn how to avoid paper cuts is a challenge. For the newly assigned Pentagon staffer it's like the Tuesday after the season's last "Monday Night Football" broadcast or the Monday after the Super Bowl—postpartum depression! First move: finding parking, then which entrance; then negotiate the maze of corridors and hallways. Walking past the first Pentagon coffee dock is a new olfactory challenge. Then, your new home, today arranged around a computer screen; my first Pentagon desk had an IBM typewriter next to it. Learning the building culture takes time and includes a course on the Program Objective Memorandum (POM) system. Go through an annual POM cycle to learn where the proverbial power is. Programs drive everything. In 1979, OP-03 was oriented on getting the Arleigh Burke Destroyer Class commissioned. But once you learn how to bob and weave through the Directorate programs, there's great satisfaction.

I consider my career mid-point in the Pentagon an "interlude." Presumably, I would get back to operations—sooner rather than later—but the new desk job was the priority. I had broad Naval Special and Surface (shipboard) Warfare experience having served on a Cruiser-Destroyer Flotilla staff, had two commands, fleet deployments including a year in Saigon, and an Attache' Tour in Phnom Penh. The challenge: garner OPNAV interest in "The Naked Warriors" and get some resources for equipment. We enjoyed some visibility in the Research and Development (R&D) world based on a couple of formal development letters oriented on demolitions and diving and getting some laboratory leverage. They provided funding for SEAL Delivery Vehicle (SDV) modifications and a suite of in-water diving gadgets—but were very constrained. In 1979, what we lacked was a universal document highlighting NSW requirements.

Summer 1982, with the master plan in the chop chain for a few weeks, I was "invited" by the detailer to return to OP-03 to assume Program Sponsorship. Part of the Pentagon culture shock is the shift from running ships, squadrons, and platoons to evaluating programs from feasibility to funding. Pentagon money is exercised within the three-phrased "Planning, Programing, and Budget System (PPBS)." The "Program Objective Memoranda (POM)" is the programmatic laydown document that starts the Five-Year Budget Cycle on its course of resource allocation. The serpentine approval path is laborious and the programs are determined by size and reviewing hosts range from the Warfare Directorates to Service Chiefs, Service Sercretariats, Defense, to Congress—all measured in billons of dollars. "Planning" (then) started the "Five-year Defense Plan (FYDP—"Fid-up")"; today it's Future Year Defense Plan," still "Fid-up." "Planning" covers the Programs the Warfare Sponsor figures are needed to do the job called out by "Defense Guidance" documents. "Programming" involves tacking dollar values to each program or line item. Funding is segregated by end use: shipbuilding, construction, operations and maintenance, research and development, military personnel, procurement, etc. (Special programs have segregated line items, like computers.) Each funding arm has rules governing spending periods; some monies are one-year funding, some two years—after which time comptrollers put on "black hats" and repossess the funds. Six months after October 1 (fiscal year), an "apportionment" drill takes place where underperforming program monies are swept up and reallocated elsewhere. I experienced this is one occasion when a SEAL Team needed five million bucks to procure upgraded communications gear; funds were shifted from the radar console of a new construction destroyer to pay for it. Ire and fumes from the OP-03 budgeteers; we collected around the conference table and we were discussing a real resource scrub to determine if the funds would be transferred. I held my ground and had the original memo from OP-06, Plans and Operations Directorate, signed out by Vice Admiral Carl Trost (later CNO). "Hmmm," I suggested, "let's cut through the chaff and walk down the 'E" Ring and ask Admiral Trost if he was serious." Spruggle, spruggle, hand wringing, hemming and hawing. We got our dough. Such encounters, happily, were rare. Other occasions occurred during the remaining POM cycles I was involved with, but armed with our 1982 Master Plan and the Thayer 1983 memo, I did as well had I found the Lost Ark of the Covenant.

Maynard Weyers did a great job in his OP-372 tour getting new small arms and closed-circuit SCUBA gear. Each set of procurements needed a separate resource briefing for a gaggle of three-stars. Nerve wracking but Captain Weyers carried the day. We obtained authority to solicit for an entire suite of small arms and a new closed circuit oxygen SCUBA family. German firms won both, respectively, Heckler and Koch (H.K.) and *Draeger*. Reminds me of a later event at a Special Operations Command business expo in Tampa. When pitching SEAL Team needs, I asked the crowd when American Industry was going to help out? To wit: we dive German 02 SCUBA, shoot German small arms (pistols and machine guns), Austrian pistols, and ride into the beach in French Combat Rubber Raiding Craft (ZODIAC). I ended by noticing that "Juan Valdez" warms our wetsuits in cold water (drink the coffee for the effect of warm urine!)

I was in the sponsor seat (recoded OP-371, Naval Special Warfare) in the summer of 1982 when the Naval Special Warfare Master Plan (NSWMP), signed out by Vice Admiral Lee Baggett, OP-095, found my "in" basket. What a relief! This plan laid out a stream of "goals and objectives" throughout the Five Year Development Plan (FYDP). That fall we were in the middle of preparing POM 95 (three years distant from 1982). My IBM now came in handy. I wrote my NSW POM input in "NARM Data Entry Sheet" format, typed with the accompanying statement typed at the bottom of the computer form: "This is Naval Special Warfare Master Plan Goal." The mists of time cloud specific memory of success. I do remember getting "SEAL Team EIGHT" into the FY-88 out-year. (Don't ask what "NARM" stands for; it was the computer format for listing POM submissions maybe "Navy Automated Resources Memoranda.") But the Master Plan approval chopped by every "E" Ring potentate, carried a certain pananche with the OP-03 POM Tsar.

Spring 1983, POM 85 in the hopper, the DESSERT ONE disaster still had SOF grieving. I had an office visit from DoD staffer,

Lynn Rynn Rylander, whom I knew. Lynn worked for Noel Koch, who reported to Assistant Secretary Richard Armitage. Lyn asked me how we had done in POM 85. I laid out a list of approved issues. I sensed Lynn was looking for failure. He announced that DoD was going to revitalize SOF in POM 86; I also got the impression they were trying to get SOF healthy in one fiscal year. Yowie, I'm in the program job less than a year but understood nothing gets funded and done in a year. I got a blank sheet of Xerox paper and did a time-dollar "X/Y" graph with a 45-degree slope modified with some easy dips, but generally positive through FY-90. I explained: (1) Laboratories are already ceilinged out with engineers working on approved programs; (2) The POM dollar flow would take six months to find Service comptrollers, who are anxious to "tax" SpecOps accounts; (3) It takes time to execute contracts—which no Service was postured to execute a ton of dough dumped on them; (4) R&D wizards need time to digest, SOF requirements, i.e., the learning curve; (5) And you simply cannot spend (execute) a lot of money and defend it in one (or two) years. I concluded by stating his funding chart needed to extend through FY-90. The resultant October 3, 1983 memo stated: "Necessary force structure expansion and enhancements in command and control, personnel policy, training, and equipment will be implemented as rapidly as possible and will be fully implemented not later than the end of fiscal year 1990." Three more paragraphs discussed collateral issues, resource sufficiency, and manpower management. The memo also made it clear that once Special Operations funding was in place, only the secretary could change it. This directive, signed out by Deputy Secretary of Defense Paul Thayer, went to all Services and DoD agencies and Services and had the effect of smacking a hornet's nest.

At this point I want to laud the Herculean efforts of Noel Koch and his staff to bring SOF issues front and center. Even with his (Thayer's) October 1983 directive, Service intransigence continued. Happily, Navy had a step by a year with our 1982 NSWMP. Lynn arranged for me to meet Noel and explain the plan. He was delighted and suggested other Service SOF jump on board and craft one. I don't recall this actually happening, but momentous sub-rosa events were taking place on the hill in the Senate. 1983 through 1986—and obviously continuing today—was a dynamic period in the maturation of SOF from the standpoints of funding, mission, and manpower. (The book to read is Susan L. Marquis's *Unconventional Warfare: Rebuilding U.S. Special Operations Forces*, Brookings Institution Press, 1997). As Marquis noted, Congressional support was growing on the hill as a result of Representative Dan Daniels and his HASC staffer, former Special Forces operator Ted Lunger. "Daniel and Lunger became the relentless force behind congressional concern for SOF throughout the 1980s."

In the meantime, Koch and Rylander were stoking the fires at the Defense Department. Without their selflessness the department would have snuffed out the vestigial commitment to SOF revitalization. In the end, the battles took the fight out of Koch who resigned (1986) and, later claimed the life of a disappointed Lynn Rylander, who died from heart attack. I might add here that the engagement overflowed the Pentagon. As it festered in Congress, it caught the attention of Ben Schemmer, editor of *Armed Forces Journal International*, whose caustic articles were digested by Congress. The Senate took the battle to heart and legislated the establishment of the U.S. Special Operations Command headquartered in MacDill Air Force Base, Tampa, Florida. Much of the credit has to go to Koch and his gang. The in-fighting was intense, dynamic, and tempestuous.

That fall, the entire OP-03 Surface Warfare directorates were told to present their FY-86 POMs to Vice Admiral Bob Walters on a Saturday morning. The DoD revitalization directive had been out a month. That memo and our Master Plan were reinforcing documents. A significant direction was to improve SOF manpower posture. For us SEALs this meant more meat on the support skeleton by way of improved technical support for electronics and associated equipment. A typical fault SEALs exhibit is downplaying the contribution these technicians and associated specialties bring to the NSW table. From founding in 1943 to post-Vietnam, SEALS wore Navy ratings and maintained most of the operating equipment—time consuming and becoming more "technical" with radios and electronics. Our POM that year was targeted to bringing fleet technicians into SEAL Teams and Boat Units. SEALs jokingly refer to non-SEALs as "admin pukes"—pretty much like Army paratroopers referring to the rest of the world as "legs." So, at my turn to brief the Admiral on the FY-87 Naval Special Warfare POM, I alluded to our personnel plus-up as affording increased administrative billets to the Teams. You'd think I had insulted him! "Admin? You just got half your submit!" I explained, "Admiral, we consider non-SEALs 'admin pukes,' but these billets are for intensive, sensitive electronics and cryptology systems." Further discourse explained how the technician growth was a Master Plan objective supported by the Defense Revitalization directive. Walking down the hall afterward guys laughed and said, "Pretty funny, George, called OP-03 and Admin Puke and got your POM." That was sufficient reward for my ego.

Later, during 1984, in the midst of the raucous DoD SOF revitalization drill, all SOF Service Program Sponsors were invited to pitch their programs to the Service Chiefs in "The Tank," the Joint Chief of Staff's conference room. As nerve wracking as this may seem, it was a unique opportunity to have your program shine. I had a set of action viewgraphs showing SEALs locking out underwater from nuclear submarines (the CNO was a "nuke"), SEALS skydiving with full equipment kit, SEALs operating in Central America, small arms and demolitions. Each presenter had twenty minutes with Q&A. After the introductions the stage fright was over and everyone did well. The Services silently went into low hovers on execution to the consternation of Noel Koch.

More on program defense: the Medium SEAL Support Craft (MSSC). For years following Vietnam, SEALs bemoaned the lack of a vessel dedicated to transport and support of Naval Special Warfare. During riverine operations in Vietnam, SEALs operated from a variety of craft like the "Monitors," landing craft refurbished with armor and guns. The Navy developed a "Medium SEAL Support Craft (MSSC)," which was a huge improvement for insertions. But after the conflict, the transport gap remained. In 1984, an Operational Requirement (OR) was submitted calling for a "Medium SEAL Support Craft"; one might argue whether or not it was too "medium" or "heavy," inasmuch as it called for a 1,500 mile endurance—750 n.m. out and back. The Surface Warfare saw no threat to their programs, and the limited number of craft was not viewed as a budget buster. The Naval Sea System architects got to work and designed an air cushion craft, a hundred feed overall. It needed "E" Ring approval to include it in a POM—my job was to get it. Quick recount: I was to present a brief to the Directors of Surface Warfare (Walters, OP-03), Plans and Operations (Trost, OP-06), and Naval Warfare (Baggett, OP-095) on an afternoon at 1500—a rare event that a sponsor brief such as an audience *in camera*. I had briefing "bullets" and a chart of the Mediterranean. I had a fresh white shirt, shined shoes, a recent haircut, and a shave. Ready. The brief was the four of us, no aides or not-takers—a captain and three vice admirals. I presented the history and list of approvals then spread a Med chart on top of the briefing table and described a transit from Naples to Libya to launch some sort of amphibious insertion. Visualize, if you will, three naval potentates bent over a chart with dividers and parallel-ruler judging the course. Walters and Baggett were Surface Warfare types, Trost a nuke submariner. Walters and Baggett smoked—reminding me of early sixties CIC enclosures with smoke and ash on radar repeaters and charts, or a mid-watch on the bridge with the tale-tale track of a lit Camel visible in the green gloom of scopes. The bosses poured over the track for thirty minutes. I stressed the point that with our own surface craft SEALs could do a mission without drawing on the Sixth Fleet for an LST or destroyer—LST hulls reserved for Marines, destroyers for carrier and surface strike missions. Total time: one hour—project approved. The regrettable end was total failure due to the contractor siphoning funds for other projects; they went out of business. The good news was several years later we got approval to construct a new class of patrol craft built Bollinger in New Orleans: CYCLONE Class Coastal Patrol Boats (PBC), 180-ft., 300 tons, launched in 1992, fourteen built. They were ostensibly replacements for the 65-foot PB MK III. Time has come for a replacement. Naval Special Warfare was deployed with a need for surface support.

The Naval Special Warfare Training Command

My third major sponsor initiative was to get CNO permission to establish a Naval Special Warfare Training Command. History refresher: Prior to 1970 Basic Underwater Demolition Team training was conducted in Little Creek, Virginia, and Coronado, California. SEAL training was for many years carried out at SEAL

Teams ONE and TWO. It was later run by the Groups, later still, all collected in the Naval Special Warfare Center responsible for Basic and SEAL Qualification Training (SQT), after which a man graduates with full SEAL Team authorization to wear the breast insignia. Before all this amalgamation, the basic course was under the Amphibious School as a subordinate department headed by a Lieutenant Commander (04). I felt for awhile that training had matured to a point justifying a discrete Commanding Officer. In addition to the Basic Course, follow-on training had developed since Vietnam. For years and years we had used other Service schools and courses. The community had matured. I initiated a briefing paper to my boss, OP-37, to establish a Captain (06) command of a new Naval Special Warfare Training Command. He concurred and the real ink was laid down on all concerned agencies—Bureau of Naval Personnel, Navy Training Command, OPNAV codes, and later when finally authorized, full-power sit-down briefings for the Chief of Naval Operations and Secretary of the Navy. I briefed the CNO (Admiral James Watkins). My relief (Captain Ted Grabowsky) got the SECNAV pitch wherein John Lehman expanded the title to "Center of Excellence." Backing up, the staffing task was building out an expanded training command apart from the Amphibious School would require cadre—instructors who came from the operating force—new construction of barracks and classrooms, training areas, that is, Niland and San Clemente Island, expanded training equipment: SCUBA, weapons, and rubber boats (IBS). New instructors needed training and movement orders, many cross-country (each coast had to support growth). I was collecting the associated planning effort as results and requirements came in. These efforts started in late 1983; the idea was to build out in calendar year 1984 and stand up the Center in 1985. This was followed. New guys came in, MILCON put up a second floor of classrooms and offices, and equipment stowage spaces. The Center opened under command of Captain Larry Bailey with a ceremony honoring retired Captain Phil Bucklew, World War II Scouts and Raiders hero and who was the Group Commander when I was Executive Officer of UDT-11.

Training has advanced. At a point further down the timeline a recent Center SQT graduation program highlights some of the training rigors, quoted here:

- Each student completed a minimum of 53 cumulative weeks of high risk training.
- Each student ran approximately 2,000 miles through time runs, conditioning runs, and other evolutions.
- Each student swam 150 miles.
- Each student ran the obstacle course approximately 41 times.
- Each student hiked/patrolled over 150 miles during training.
- Each student conducted at least 42 dives while spending a minimum of 62 (or 2.5 days) under the water on dive status.
- The class expended over 1,415 rounds of small arms ammunition.
- The class detonated 13,384 lbs. of high explosives.
- Class 302 has done the equivalent of swimming from Cuba to the southern tip of Florida, then running to New York City. (No information on who will pay for the keg of beer on Rockaway Beach, Long Island.)

What the above standards don't mention is the exuberant exhorts from accompanying instructors or the climatic environment of Southern California-like cold ocean, rain (rare), wind (always), time of day (24/7), wet clothes, sand, lack of sleep, outside temperature, soft sand dunes, high surf. Training has evolved since my 1965 Class 36!

The Center was approved, and training has matured over the years to a world class endeavor. Another huge change was I had a hand in the switch over the Underwater Demolition Teams to SEAL and SEAL Delivery Vehicle (SDV) Teams, circa 1983. The idea wasn't mine. Cathal "Irish" Fynn, then Commander Naval Special Warfare Group ONE, suggested the name change at an annual "Cross-tell" conference, that year held in Arlington. There was lively discussion from which a unified concurrence surfaced. As the OPNAV program sponsor, I pointed out that each group needed to come into OPNAV via the Fleets' chain of command, couching the initiative as a "name change." New establishment of a command requires Congressional approval and thirty-day posted notice. The reality would be an increase in the Table of Organizational Equipment (TOE), which costs would need POM development. Happily-thrice over-timing was with us by dint of DoD revitalization initiative. The bulk-up of gear developed fairly smoothly.

My time in OPNAV was running out. One event told me how we were doing: at a come-as-you-are budget dump to the Deputy OP-03 Directorate, Rear Admiral David Altweg (RIP). I had my NAVSEA spending pitch of viewgraphs in hand ready for presentation. I sat through the ship driver codes speaking from envelops; I had our NAVSEA officer pitch our fully-funded PO. Admiral Altweg spoke, "We can't lose a dime of Naval Special Warfare programs." I think I blushed.

An interesting note, Washington being political has elections. The year 1980 was a victory for Ronald Reagan. The days leading up to the inauguration put on galas and parties. Supporting one of their own, Hollywood luminaries descended on Washington en masse. The Pentagon was a rare source for escorts; I was assigned to Debbie Reynolds and her friend, a Texas oilman and former

WW II Air Corps fighter pilot. Ms. Reynolds is well-known to at least two generations of film goers. On one of her Korean War USO trips, she was shot down behind enemy lines; her brother was a seriously wounded Army grunt. She was the emcee at the Watergate to introduce Barbara Bush to an audience. We arrived at the theater thirty minutes before the ceremony. She sat down with a 3x5 note card and pencil and jotted her points down, curtain call; it's like she rehearsed her pitch for a month. I couldn't give a Pentagon briefing without a viewgraph slide! She was engaging and interesting. I escorted them in the Pentagon assigned sedan for four days, which included the dinner before the inaugural, with Frank Sinatra, and the inaugural itself the next day. Following the swearing in, we piled on a bus with a dozen showbiz stars and went to the next event. It was winding down. Whew.

Four years later, another election needing manpower. I was selected, without input, to head up the OPNAV contingent to march down Pennsylvania Avenue, sword, etc. The weather was not cooperating. The day of the rehearsal was conducted in zero-degree weather. Dressed warm. I wore black jump boots and several layers of clothes. We dutifully marched down Pa. Ave. Brrr. Insult to injury. I was coming down with the crud, a worse cold I've rarely had. The temperature was plummeting. Doug Flutie was throwing Heisman passes to his roommate, Gerard Phalen. Then the announcement: the inaugural parade scheduled for tomorrow is cancelled. "Hail to the Chief!" That was the most welcomed news I'd ever had. My life was spared.

On a more personal level, during my first OPNAV assignment, I got married (1981) and welcomed two of my three children, two boys born at Bethesda (1982 and 1984). My departure from Washington headed West to command of Naval Special Warfare Group ONE in

Coronado. But what'd learn from six years in the Pentagon on two Navy staffs? Wow! Looking back I think I learned that using the system is more effective than bucking it trying to find shortcuts. One thing I observed was time in the building helped with the process such as identifying a problem or issue or initiative, and getting the right staff directorate to help was essential. People on a "chop" chain love to be included in the solution, especially the higher up. One progress I've cited a couple of in the fray issues—getting a SEAL boat and getting the training command commissioned. I also learned that scribbling my POM issues on a scrap of paper never worked. I type my input in the desired computer format and got it in early. Never failed . . . as my final example explains, blushing notwithstanding.

What'd I learn six years in the building? The first thing I observe was be nice to the civilians. You don't win your case pissing people off, and as I learned working with Ms. Goldberg, a cup of coffee can win a lot of support. Next, don't waste time trying to end run the administrative wickets; if all the chop blocks are initialed, you win. Next, have your facts—you gotta pass the proverbial smell test. Next, be mature in your pursuits. If the budget ax comes your way, be graceful in acceptance; come reapportionment you might get stuffed back. Back to the "chop blocks." Nothing succeeded more than our Master Plan. The fact that it was sponsored by OP-095 got the "E" Ring attention. As long as other code dollars were not highlighted, no one would disagree. Of course, OP-095 didn't have money; OP-03 would have to assume a bill. That got us squarely a seat in the POM process . . . final and before the DoD revitalization memo hit the street. We were ahead of the game. Learning point: get out first.

PENTAGON INTERLUDE PHOTO

July 1985, end-of-tour award for six years on the Navy Staff (OPNAV) presented by Vice Admiral Joe Metcalf, USN, Assistant Chief of Naval Operations for Surface Warfare: first tour was in OP-37(Amphibs, Mines, EOD, Specwar) 1979–1980; a tour in OP-954 (published a Master Plan) 1980–1982; final tour again as OP-371 (stand-alone Naval Special Warfare Directorate—a one-man shop!).

CHAPTER 13

MAJOR COMMAND: 1985-1987

My Pentagon interlude concluded—six years in the building—I had orders for my "06" Major Command: Naval Special Warfare Group ONE, Naval Amphibious Base, Coronado, California—home to my previous two commands, SEAL Team ONE and Inshore Undersea Warfare Group ONE.

I had worked my entire Naval Special Warfare career under the leadership of Group ONE—Captains Phil Bucklew, Bob Stanton, Frank Kaine, Dave Schaible, John O'Drain and more with my contemporaries, "Irish" Fllynn and Chuck Le Moyne, whom I would soon replace. NSWG-1 reported to Commander Naval Surface Force, U.S. Pacific Fleet, at that time Vice Admiral Harry Schrader, my first boss in OP-37. We were well acquainted with each other. Our Change of Command took place that summer. Chuck went back to Washington on orders to the Strategic Study Group (SSG) that worked directly under the Chief of Naval Operations (CNO). Guys selected to the SSG worked a year on a task given by the Service Chief. All were considered "Water Walkers"; few failed to select to Flag. I suspected I was safe, although I enjoyed my time in Washington and the Pentagon.

As a brief postscript to the previous chapter, life at that period was exciting in the Pentagon. Special Operations were undergoing a colossal refurbishing, as I discussed. Special Ops people were making an impact on all Services, not that everyone on those staffs were excited about. The Pentagon runs on money. Some guy gets it, someone loses—"Zero Sum Game" with finite numbers. Riding on the impression of our Master Plan, SEALs were doing comparatively better than brother soldiers and airmen. This is not to chortle, we dipped oars into the rolling joint waters alongside the rest; we just, initially, had more to show for our progress than the others. I worked three POM submits for 100 percent approval and the result includes efforts by Maynard Weyers and Dick Marcinko. We added SEAL Teams EIGHT and SIX and commissioned the Naval Special Warfare Center as a Major Captain command. Weyers succeeded acquiring new diving equipment and the H&K submachinegun suite. Group TWO tested out a lightweight M-60 machinegun that NAVSEA approved. Life on the Navy Staff was fulfilling.

Getting back to Coronado after seven years in Washington was thrilling, too, especially for the kiddos. We arrived with two boys; a girl came in 1986. Small town Coronado has one of the finest beaches in America. The school system remains superior. The Pacific Command offered unlimited opportunity to train and interact with allies. I participated in numerous combined exercises from the Philippines to Thailand to Malaysia to Korea. We even had a SEAL officer stationed at Chinhae Naval Base in addition to Naval Special Warfare Unit ONE in Subic Bay; and not to overlook our SEAL officer with Commander SEVETH Fleet, which relationship became cautionary as a result of SEAL Team operational responsibilities to the PACOM Joint Special Operations Task Group operating out of the PACOM staff. We had a billet on the Pacific Fleet Staff too. But they were tied to Hawaii. I was free to travel wherefrom I had access to the joint operators and NAVFORKOREA War Plans, which covered more than definitive SEVENTH Fleet OPLANs. We had a "Purple Uniform" platoon that could operate beyond COMSEVENTHFLT Operational Command or Control—a continuing source of friction. I had to walk a narrow path. I routinely called on C7F in his flagship after laborious explanation to "our guy" on the staff. Not sure I ever made a dent. (That specific admiral, Vice Admiral Paul McCarthy (RIP), retired in Coronado, and we got along fine.) I was delicately skirting the boundaries of command prerogatives owing to the long-term condition of jointly-assigned SEALs. Navy always appeared jealous of forces—who owns what and under what span of control, I was a judicious subordinate. It was certainly more comfortable on the Navy Staff; your "buttons" identified your position on staff and in the joint spaces. It was much more complicated "down range" in Thailand at the fishing villages.

The travel was taxing on the family. In any quarter I could be TAD/TDY twenty-one days, plus or minus. There were fleet and joint exercises, inspections, travel to schmooze, occasional calls in the Pentagon and at the Bureau of Naval Personnel. Then the important "cross-tell conferences" with Naval Special Warfare Group TWO and our OPNAV directorate—to argue about the budget—and that other example of changing UDTs into SEAL Teams, discussed earlier. With the "Revitalization of Special Operations" effort maturing, we were faring well on finances. The Navy's angst was how all the jointness would affect fleet operations—would the Amphibs lose their SEAL recon platoons? What would Navy have to do, ask the Army for a recon platoon? Well, yes, it got ridiculous; but in the event the Amphib Ready Group got its SEAL platoon seamlessly! USCOCOM wasn't about to insert himself into fleet makeup—that wasn't General Jim Lindsay's "MO." A more reasonable man I have yet to meet. But these Service fears were only simmering when I took command in 1985. They started in the wake of the Iran hostage attempt and hit the proverbial front burner with Noel Koch's revitalization memorandum signed out to services and agencies by DEPSECDEF Paul Thayer. Until 1987 we operated under Navy Operational Command and Fleet Operational Control (OPCON). Congressional legislation made it change over to U.S. Special Operations Command with an administrative link to Service Chiefs. On the waterfront, the Amphibious Forces got their SEALs just like before. If you crack the pages of defense funding, one learns the Services still foot a huge tab for their Special Operations Forces (SOF). Military Construction (MILCOM), personnel (MILPERS), air frames—fixed and rotary wing—ships and transport (trucks and tanks), health (which includes families), guns and ammo/demolitions. The stand-alone USSOCOM budget, Title ELEVEN, is for "SOF Unique" material and equipment. My tenure at NSWG-1 was all Navy funded. In fact, it took SOCOM a couple of years to come to grips with all the cross-walking of funding and developing intelligent POM submissions. Well, in General Stiner's tour he discovered that Army had not transferred rotary wing funding.

Back to the job at NSWG-1. In addition to providing SEALs and special boats throughout the Pacific Command, principally to Commander SEVENTH Fleet, we also had responsibility to the Middle East and Africa—all of them. We did exercises with Jordan and Kenya. By comparison, NSWG-2 had responsibility for Latin America, the Caribbean, and Europe (including Nordic and Mediterranean). Enough work for four Groups. The legislation stood up flag officer commands in the special operations area command staffs: SOCEUR, SOCCENT, SOCPAC, and SOCKOREA.

We did an exercise with the Jordanian coast guard. They were energetic and eager to learn. I had a diesel engine tech along with the Special Boat Unit, a Senior Chief Petty Officer. One morning we passed by Jordanian boat *pukka*, and there was the chief, cap askew, arms coated in grease—a scene from "McHale's Navy!" He personally overhauled all the coast guard patrol boats—bringing them back to 30-knot speeds. The diving locker needed more attention.

In Kenya, we worked with the Kenyan Navy diving command. They rarely went on night ops—"Simba." Lots of snakes in Kenya too. And forget about swimming outside the lagoon—sharks. But we enjoyed the hospitality of both countries. Nairobi was a welcoming environment, some English pubs. Jordan was more cautious, less smiles, no English pubs. No "bashing gin and tonic." As military readers may appreciate, all these multi-continent exercises from Asia to Africa to the Middle East—and those going down I CONUS with travel and training—all added up to time away from home port. It's estimated we were on the road over 60 percent of a year gone. And compare that to the recent deployments to Afghanistan and Iraq, a template overlay to necessary out-of-town training— sniper school, cold weather training, local ranges (overnight duty), off-shore demolition work (San Clemente Island). The impact on SEAL Team families has been, and continues to be, arduous. Half a dozen deployments have meant years away from growing families. Then the deaths and wounded . . . and Congress wants to cut benefits—and the president reputed to have wanted the wounded to pay their own medical bills. Who speaks for us?

More on exercises—*Foal Eagel in Korea:* we were able to deploy the Group Mobile Communications Team (MCT) to Chinhae— first time overseas in a major joint exercise. The Korean Navy gave us a soccer field to set up. The C3 van had wires strung out to an adjacent Tactical Ops Center (TOC) in a tent. A low frequency long-wire antenna was arrayed over the field. We could have communicated with Mars! We had links to Hawaii, the Coronado Strand (HQ), and all exercise players to include SEAL platoons in the field. It was superb—all following a decade of development; the capability was a mature addition to Naval Special Warfare. No longer necessary to pick up traffic from the "Army-Air Force Message Center." No longer necessary to endure joint logistics supply lines; simply fire a message request back home and a piece of gear could leave North Island Naval Air Station within twenty-four hours. Okay, longer if we needed something from St. Louis, but the Service hassle was partially eliminated. And the mobile network afforded timely post-op radio updates. As I've alluded to earlier, today fifty tons of comm gear aboard a C5 aircraft deploy the MCT today.

1985–1987 went by fast. We did countless briefings, deployments, demonstrations, and policy papers. We worked the budget issues as only someone with six years in the Puzzle Palace can. I knew the end user in OP-37. After I took over the Group, I followed up on my initiative to commission the NSW School. Secretary Lehman had expanded the issue to become a "center of excellence." My last briefing before detaching from OOPNAV was before CNO Jim Watkins. He approved and moved it to the SECNAV decision desk. To ensure that the manpower lever was poised to drop, I had my Chief Staff Officer, Commander Tom Lawson (Ranger School grad and Vietnam Purple Heart recipient), hop on the red eye that evening back to D.C. in civvies to go into the OP-37 SEAL archive; and pull out the personnel action paper and deliver it to the OP-39 (Surface Warfare) action officer's *pukka* and place it on his desk. That done, the personnel system had to absorb . . . and it did. Navy commissioned the center in 1986 and named it after Captain Phil Bucklew. As a center, it overseas the basic SEAL and Special Boat courses and numerous advanced courses. It is a major command today.

Spring 1987, my tenure at the helm of NAVSPECWARGRU ONE was closing down timewise. A mid-summer turnover was on the horizon. Captain Ted Grabowsky was my nominal relief. I had orders for a follow-on command tour to relieve Captain Larry Bailey as C.O. of the Center. I was delighted! Then a fly in the ointment. Rear Admiral Le Moyne was contacted by the BUPERS assignment desk seeking a replacement for a Chief of Staff to Special Operations Command Europe in Stuttgart. (Actually, it's on Patch Barracks, Vaihingen, then West Germany.) Le Moyne, without calling me, offered me. This three weeks before the announced change of command, invites were already sent out. I got a phone call from the detailer, a classmate. My orders had been changed, I was on my way to Germany. I caught Le Moyne with chicken feathers all over his lips! After several *mea culpas,* he tried explaining how important it was to fill joint billets. I knew the routine and recognized how futile it would be to fight City Hall. The hard part was breaking the news to my family, who were looking forward to some tranquility. Not to happen. I left for *Deutschland* unaccompanied. My SSOCEUR tour was destined to be short, so I'll tack in on here.

Before deploying that September, I felt it important to check in with Ft. Bragg Special Forces people, specifically Generals Joe

Lutz and Sid Shacknow. They afforded staff briefings on happenings in EUCOM. These were important contacts. Brigadier Terry Scott was the SOCEUR Commander. Scott, a Texas A&M alum and Ranger, was selected flag out of PACOM. He knew the Army ropes and was direct and determined. He was later selected three-stars and headed up USASOC. My arrival put a clink in the SOCEUR chain of command. It seems I was senior to the deputy, an Air Force colonel. I waved a glove over the error and elected not to upset the functioning arrangement. I got along fine with the staff, mostly Army, a Navy SEAL (whom I knew when he was enlisted petty officer on my team), and a Marine Corps major. We had several enlisted staffers headed up by an E7 Sergeant or "top." It was enlightening to learn the inner workings of a huge joint staff. The overall EUCOM command was situated in Le Mons, Belgium. The Deputy EUCOM at Vaihingen was an Air Force general. The J3 operations was a Navy Rear Admiral. All Service representatives were sprinkled throughout the humongous community. Patch Barracks was a community in effect and spirit. I was the senior "06" on post awaiting quarters. I was living out of the Post Hotel a.k.a. BOQ. Before this tour the bulk of my Special Operations deployment experience was in Asia excepting the Mid-East/Africa exercises and administrative "touch downs" in London and Paris. It was eye-opening, to say the least. First trip out of town was a trip to Garmisch to palaver with the Army Special Forces detachment—learning more every day. Beyond developing staff capability monitoring EUCOM SOF employment, we got involved with "real world" events, which is not to suggest monitoring exercises does not require real effort. Some of the exercise drills involved host countries' clandestine services—without putting too fine a point on it. Our Marine was point of contact for agency issues. We also had responsibility for Special Operations plans in EUCOM War Plans.

Tuesday, December 15, 1987, I got a phone call from Margaret Fuller, our community's officer detailer in BUPERS, announcing my selection to Flag. Well, what a grand shock—I'm sure for the community too. (It was afternoon in Arlington.) It does no revelation wondering why so and so gets promoted and so and so didn't. We had several officers who could have made it. I might have selected a couple others. But done is done. Several days later, I found, myself with General Scott standing at the elbow of the CINC Army General John Galvin. Scott introduced me with the news of my promotion at which General Galvin erupted with false discouragement that damned Navy never sends officers for full tours—all in exaggerated good humor. What he did command of us was the capability to report Soviet red tail lights heading west. Early warning, I guess. Right ... we'll be able to do that next week.

Another tasking came to SOCEUR from the joint chiefs of staffs in the Pentagon. Come up with a plan to locate Marine Colonel William R. Higgins, kidnapped by Hezbollah in 1988. The Joint Special Operations Command sent a joint contingent of officers to assist in the planning. This was a highly visible undertaking. Time was limited, urgency was paramount, the evening wick burned brightly. Regretfully, the ink couldn't dry fast enough. Higgins was murdered—a year short of thirty years ago, and I'll bet there are still Marines ready to avenge his death. Of course, looking back, wasn't that a glimpse of things to come?

One afternoon, I got a phone call from Brigadier General Wayne Downing, director of the USSOCOM Pentagon liaison office. He announced that General Lindsay wanted me for the newly legislated Special Operations-Law Intensity Conflict in the Defense Staff.

Would I agree? I made some lighthearted crude response, which amounted to "delighted." Two weeks the secretary of the Army, John Marsh, dropped by our staff offices to get a look at me, as I would be working for him as acting SOLIC. "Where were you born, son?"

"Louisville, Kentucky, Sir." So far so good. We chatted a few minutes. I later had to run by the Secretary of the Navy and Chief of Naval Operations, Jim Webb and Carlisle Trost, respectively. CNO was a stand-up pass as he ate his lunch; Webb was a thirty-minute sit-down at 1600. Cleared to attend "knife and fork" class. I was fortunate not having to attend the flag officer joint indoctrination course, KEYSTONE. SOLIC needs its own chapter, but what'd I learn from major command and a truncated European staff command?

NAVSPECWARGRU ONE allowed me to avoid the errors of my two earlier commands. One can't help but learn from experience. Well, one hopes so. I learned to bring to command attention the challenge of preparing for two commanders, naval and joint. The group command is far more expansive than a team spot. Keeping the chain of command informed was a critical lesson learned. We were developing two chains of command—the Navy Service and SOCOM—this even before the formal change of operational control (OPCON). Delft footwork is handy too, but sprinkle the same seeds on both.

Happy Hour with South Korean Navy Commandos. C.O. is to my right. Tough guys. We did several major exercises with them during which we deployed two HUEY helicopters—the inheritors of the Vietnam era Light Attack Helicopter Squadrons—Navy logistics refer to them as "Helicopter, Attack, Light (HAL)." The mountainous topography of Korea is reinforced by many high power lines, fatal to low fliers.

The annual Coronado rough water swim event-Fourth of July Celebrations.

CHAPTER 14

SOLIC DEFENSE DEPARTMENT: 1988-1989

May 1988, back in Washington to house hunt and get reacquainted with the Pentagon. How long was I gone? Three years; 1985 to command, to Stuttgart, then back . . . truly a whirlwind. Checked in with the Special Operations/Low Intensity Conflict (SOLIC) shop, at the time with acting director Army Secretary John O. Marsh. I was still wearing captain's shoulder boards. I was shortly advanced "frocked" in Marsh's office under the famous painting of Washington at Valley Forge—probably the first Navy guy promoted by the Army Secretary Marsh for a shot. There was a slight connection. Marsh had been a Northern Virginia member of Congress; my ole' man, a 1932 graduate of the University of Virginia.

Now, the challenge of stirring the building dust to furrow out a staff habitat. At that time we were satellite stashes around the ground floor several hiking minutes away from the "Headshed," which set of spaces housed the administrative heartbeat but no formal occupant.

My alighted position was "Deputy Assistant Secretary of Defense for Special Operations"—DASDSO, I guess. I had Special Operations Forces (SOF) activities like policy, operations, programs and budgets; but no controlling authority, just readers of events. There existed a chain of command from the Secretary of Defense through the Joint Staff to the U.S. Special Operations Command (legislated by Congress in 1986). Wedging a perch somewhere in the building, pecking order required diplomacy and aplomb. One well-protected directorate was the ASD for Intelligence, very sensitive to "turf"—Charlie Hawkins I seem to remember, a good guy with skin where Intel programs were concerned—many have gone away, new ones up, all fences constructed over time with lubricated agreements.

All was well that summer. My Pentagon Officers' Athletic Club (POAC) membership was still active and the Fort Myer swimming pool was five minutes away. I also had the option of swimming with the D.C. Masters Team in the early morning (0530)—a little more difficult with three young kiddos. Every day I was able to have breakfast at the Pentagon cafeteria, which offered a delectable display of potential waist-spreading doom! There were several secretarial dining rooms available too. Did anyone ever starve to death in the Pentagon? Thank the Lord for POAC.

A major obstacle on the road to continued SOF "revitalization" was obtaining the USSOCOM stand alone budget authority, Program ELEVEN (P-11), as it was called out in legislation. The department was dragging its feet, as were all the Services. It was two years since implementation of legislation designed improve SOF. Resistance was a "Fifth Column" element that infiltrated all levels, regrettably including SOLIC. It would be a year of in-fighting get to it; it was finally approved by the Deputy SECDEF in summer 1989. The battle wasn't pretty.

Late August I was in my *Pukka* when Dick Brown walked into my office. Retired Marine Corps Lieutenant Colonel Brown was the Naval Sea Systems Command (NAVSEA) point of contract for small arms programs. I had worked with Dick when I was on the Navy staff. He handled small arms for all Naval Special Warfare accounts, SEAL and Special Boat Teams. Dick was the bearer of bad news—the new Beretta nine millimeter pistol was fragmenting; the slides were breaking off and injuring shooters. The first several at the Air Force Guard Course in Texas. He dropped information on my lap. I queried if anyone on OPNAV was addressing the problem. He said no, because it was an Army program. I suggested going to Secretary Marsh with a Point Paper explaining the problem. This I did within forty-eight hours. Marsh forwarded it to the Army Rock Island Arsenal-Joint Manufacturing & Technology Center (if I recall correctly). Within a week they came back, Admiral Worthington is all wet, blah, blah ... My first shot from my new perch went thump. What's next? Fate.

Secretary Marsh went on a field trip and was observing SEALs doing room clearance. All of a sudden, a Beretta backfired (literally, the side flies off the housing and hits shooters in the jam). Blood everywhere, in full sight of the Acting ASD Special Operations—Low Intensity Conflict—and Secretary of the Army responsible for fielding side arms to all Services. Marsh's response was out before his chopper took off. Hold further procurement of the pistols and get Beretta to fix the (seeming) design flaw. Whew! A bullet dodged ... or slide.

Secretary Marsh was famous for hosting cat fish dinners in the Army dining room, to which he would invite Congressmen for SOF briefings. These weren't drink-a-thongs; we were on duty—the fried cat fish were wonderful. I met the prospective ASD SOLIC at one of these. Former Ambassador Charles S. Whitehouse, with experience from III-Corps in Vietnam and embassy stint in Bangkok. Whitehouse was the son of a State Department diplomat and was born in Paris. A Yale grad, he took off during World War II to fly with the Marine Corps in the Pacific Theater. He had been an early roommate of Frank Carlucci, at the time Secretary Defense. Whitehouse would report to work and await Senate confirmation.

Whitehouse, who passed away in 2000, was a prince of a gentleman, genuine "old school" New England. He called the SOLIC staff together, and stressed the importance of dignity comprised of character, diligence, and rectitude—lest I sermonize. Along with these attributes are perseverance and dedication. He gave as long a leash as any action officer could wish for. He asked retired Army Major General John Murray to come on board as Principal Deputy. As we were still very much the SOF revitalization role, I brought Lynn Rylander around to meet him. (Lynn's initial boss, Noel Koch, had resigned and was replaced by Larry Ropka.) We briefed the ambassador on all the continuing in-fighting, who "the enemy" might be, and which obstacles we continued to contest. We identified the budget authorization as the biggest challenge.

We made a foreign trip to London, Paris, and Stuttgart. In London we met with the counter-terror (CT) people. Then we flew out to SAS headquarters. Next stop, France to meet CT officials— and Whitehouse spoke fluent French!—thence to watch a sniper demonstration by French shooters. Stuttgart for meetings with Deputy EUCOM and the SOCEUR staff, later with Air Force and

Army units. All this DoD attention was new for the EUCOM CT batting order, including our own American staffs. Growing pains. The principal challenge for Ambassador Whitehouse was to find a modus operandi with General Lindsay. Suffice it to say, they got along fine on a personal level, perhaps half the battle. Whitehouse had no desire to pump the numbers the Command was obliged to live with. There was one issue that was cause for concern, namely, the eventual bed-down location for new Combat Talon modified C-130 aircraft. The Air Commandos on SOLIC staff wanted squadrons at Huerlburt Field, Florida; the CINC wanted them in New Mexico. My guys were waging an unconventional warfare campaign to get them to stay in Florida. This contest pre-dated my arrival. "Found on Post" position papers had been drifting around Pentagon parking lots. Blood would soon be split. I threw a yellow flag and invited "Irish" Flynn, then, at McDill, to bring his crew to town and have it out with our detractors. I had not formed an opinion but tended toward the SOCOM position; I was disinclined to buck the Commander for fear of warping the relationship. You might see where resolution of this decision could have tainted the entire relationship between SOCOM and SOLIC. My job, as I viewed it, was to preserve the cordial relationship between the two principals. Whitehouse, at this point, probably hoped for a diplomatic outcome and not destroy the allegiance of his staff. Above all, the outcome of the bed-down issue would color all future tugs-of-war. I acquiesced in letting Flynn chair the discussion; it was their initiative. My "Air" group was driven by comfort considerations, like twenty-five cent Gulf oysters. Albuquerque, New Mexico, offered far more challenging geographic-topography for Combat Talon training. (And better skiing in winter; so the oysters cost more.) We scrapped through with the decision to uphold the CINC's position. A month later

I went out to Albuquerque to see the base and meet the people in charge—one of whom was Colonel Charlie Holland, a future SOCOM commander. (I was able to make a static-line parachute jump from a helicopter—made the trip worthwhile.)

The downside of my fall season that election year (1988) was the surprise passing of my father in Tucson, just before the election. He would have voted for Bush. It was a sorrowful Thanksgiving. The event bypassed the kids' cognizance. We simply told them, "Granny Bo went to heaven." He was seventy-seven but had undergone quad- bypass surgery for years before. "LSMFT" gets 'em in the end. From my days in Rockaway, I recall the Camel smoke ring machine on Times Square puffing out smoke circles into the New York air. Oh, yes, LSMT meant "Lucky Strike Means Fine Tabaco"— an oxymoron. A few years before he passed away, he and mother took a trip to Russia. Dad had grown up with the Russians in the news as social and economic examples—much of the praise later debunked. *New York Times* reported Walter Duranty's lavished erroneous praise on Stalin. But they enjoyed themselves. Dad was with an Alcohol Anonymous group and later remarked how the Russian wives would flood him with questions about how they could get their husbands sober.

Our push to get the CINC his budget became cantankerous— among us staffers too. I suspected an internal effort to obstruct the effort—naming no names. It was public knowledge Defense wasn't anxious to cough up a pile of cash by a levy against Service budgets. But, most of us argued, the legislation was clear on this matter. Incidentally, Whitehouse didn't just get off the bus. After his confirmation, Senator McCain spoke with him, and dumped the essence of a recent SOCLIC staff meeting. QED. Happily, we prevailed and Deputy Secretary of Defense William Taft authorized the stand-alone USSOCOM Major Force Program (MFP-11). Of course, detractors still harrumph that the Services still pick up a good deal of the SOF tab—as I eluded to earlier: MILCON, Medical, Aircraft, Personnel (pay and retirement benefits, *inter alia*).

Early Spring, 1979, then, SOCOM CINC, General Lindsay, pulled me aside and announced quietly that he needed a new budget guy. The only one inside the SOCOM constellation of stars that met that dollar standard was Rear Admiral Chuck Le Moyne, the current COMNAVSPECWAR with a Master's Degree in financial management and career-wide experience matching budgets and operational requirements. Would I be open to relieving Chuck that summer? (Duh!) Sir, I'd be honored and delighted. Chuck and I had followed each other's wakes for several commands. He would have been in command two years, normally a year short, but needs of the service prevail and with recent SOCOM command experience and that degree, no other choice remained with General Lindsay. So, July it was to be. My replacement was Marine Corps Brigadier General Charlie Wilhelm, who went on to four stars and geographic command of SOUTHCOM. The new administration was in place, too, and Ambassador Whitehouse was looking forward to relaxing on the Northern Virginia "Hunt." His relief was named Senate Staffer Jim Locher, a West Point graduate and chief architect of the Goldwater-Nichols Act—a better choice at the time was hard to find. To criticize Locher as a pure policy wonk would do him injustice; he had a firm understanding of military strategy and, yes, policies necessary to accomplish same. His arrival strengthened the SOLIC Directorate. The CINC had his budget—not to say the battles were over!—the Deputy Assistant Secretary infrastructure had matured, the 1983 Defense "Special Operations Revitalization" initiative had taken hold, the black birds weren't circling over career cadavers, and SEALs were not looked down on come flag promotion board time. (I will have more to comment on this next chapter.)

What'd I learn in SOLIC? First flag tour: keep your eyes and ears open and mouth closed. Most experience would accrue from Navy and Joint Staff (EUCOM) exposure. The former was determined by POM success; the latter by Force Planning acumen (adroit recommendations on Service integration in war plans). On SOLIC success was contingent on bringing the SOF capabilities in line with Congressional Legislation. Other DoD agencies might object to this or that initiative. It remained to be polite and point out the law without pissing someone off-leave a diplomatic opening for the combative directorate to gain some praise fulfilling the law. It served well to highlight a particular agency's assistance on matters; joyful assistance was recorded up the chain; recalcitrance invited the spotlight of nefarious suspicion. I was on my way to a (as it turned out) three-year flag tour.

SOLIC PHOTOS

Secretary of the Army John O. March promoting me to the rank of Rear
Admiral (lower half) and passing a Secretary of Defense assignment
document—under the painting of General Washington at Valley Forge.
Quite an experience. Marsh was at the time serving as Acting Assistant
Secretary of Defense for Operations and Low Intensity Conflict. My title
was Deputy Assistant Secretary of Defense (Special Operations).

CHARLES SHELDON WHITEHOUSE
November 5, 1921 – June 25, 2001

Retired Ambassador Charles S. Whitehouse was asked by Secretary Carlucci to come on board the new Directorate as Assistant Secretary; Whitehouse accepted. I met him at one of Marsh's catfish dinners. Whitehouse was a Marine Corps attack pilot in the Pacific Campaign during WW II. He left Yale for flight school. He also served as a State Department official in II Corps Vietnam and was later U.S. Ambassador to Thailand. He was a Hunt Chef in Virginia. He died of lung cancer in 2000.

CHAPTER 15

NAVAL SPECIAL WARFARE COMMAND: 1989-1992

Rear Admiral Chuck Le Moyne and I exchanged hand salutes on July 1989. He would be off for Tampa, Florida, headed for a "J" slot on the U.S. Special Operations Command. It would prove a propitious move for him and his experience—and of course selection to Upper Half, our community's first. A new era was unfolding for Naval Special Warfare officers.

My first order of official business was to ponder replacements for lead staff members slated for new orders. The Command Headquarters were temporarily sited in slick vans south of the Coronado shores condominiums on the beach side of the Naval Amphibious Base. Construction of a permanent building was about eight months from completion. My first nominee was for a Flag Lieutenant-Aide. I asked for a woman. Navy approved and sent a lieutenant. She never travelled with me but was in charge of my social calendar and flag visits—plus, the hard part, deciphering temporary additional duty travel—always coach except on that rare occasion a flight crew would upgrade my Command Master Chief and me. Next was a Flag Writer, I kept the Petty Officer already in the job, a minority female who did a splendid job. The Command staff had a good number of females. The senior budget person was a GS15 woman with years of experience. She was a hold-over . . . or was pleased to stay. Staff jobs in the Service are not political. The flag officer's personal staff can be rotated—up to the incumbent. I was satisfied with the people. We had good diversity back when it wasn't a somewhat mandatory consideration. I had two minority people in my front office staff and plenty of women throughout the Command. (Later, our JAG officer was female.)

My first real professional challenge was training. SEALs and frogmen have been training themselves since 1943. We borrowed courses from numerous sources and sent out people to various Service schools. Then one day, at a collective SOCOM subordinate commander's meeting, General Lindsay asked me how SEALs trained—and by implication the Special Boat Squadrons. I stuttered out essentially the excuse offered by the first two sentences of this paragraph. And I had Xerox copies of an Army training course. I explained out basic underwater demolition training and follow-on workup in land warfare. It was a flimsy presentation, clearly unimpressive to the joint audience of three-star commanders. Uba-dee, uba-dee, uba-dee . . . I know I had a task in front of me. In fact the training at that time (1989) was each cost did it differently under auspices of the local Naval Special Warfare commander. Well, we had an admiral in charge of all SEALs commands; there needed to be consistency. In truth, in the days of two SEAL Teams. UDT volunteers were trained by the individual Team. When I was at NSWG-1, I saw the need for consistency that advanced training had to be coordinated at the group level, and so consistency that advanced training had to be coordinated at the group level, and so established a Group Advanced Training Cadre. But that was for the Pacific.

Now, four years later, I found myself representing both coasts and all SEAL Teams. Time to get it all under one roof! How to do it? Collect a group of experienced SEAL Team mid-grade officers and senior enlisted people together with the task of coming up with a unified training syllabus beyond the Basic Underwater Demolition/ SEAL (BUD/S) training course, which was twenty-five people representing East and West Coasts. After five days, they reported out that it couldn't be done. Hmmm. I mused, "Gentlemen, our TAD budget is extensive. We'll be here until we get it done. I want to see white smoke come out of the chimney before we break camp!" Of course I knew I was blowing smoke, but I also realized the CINC had to answer to SECDEF and the Congress. I was surprised this issue hadn't cropped up with Le Moyne. It would have come up sooner or later. In fact, Operation JUST CAUSE into Panama, December 1989, would illustrate the need for coordinated training. I am cautious to get into details of the operation; everybody performed as expected— still, there were questions about having SEALs attack Patilla Aiport. Then, the unit that held the position for some eighteen hours were to have been relieved in four by an Army battalion. "All's well that ends well." But was it worth the cost of lives for SEALs Killed in Action (KIA). Controversy will accompany any post-operation "Hot Wash." The grumbling about JUST CAUSE percolated several years. From my part, I was surprised at the level of effort expended. In fact, I had not received any general briefing on the Panama operation during my turnover before the Change of Command—security was so tight. The only hint I got was briefing by Captain Rick Woolard, Commanding Officer of "SEAL Team SIX." That brief contained nothing about any involvement by NSWG-2, yet it was two Group TWO divers who destroyed a Panama patrol boat that initiated the opening fires of the operation. I don't know for a fact that anybody on my staff had any inclination of Group TWO tasking—something to be fixed in the months to follow.

At one point after JUST CAUSE, we found ourselves in the annual laydown of a POM submission—Program Objective Memorandum, the gear and spending needing to be included. Back in the 1983–84 timeframe, I was able to plus-up the NSW manpower line on the strength of our Master Plan and the DoD Revitalization Memo. We were, for the most part, neophytes when it came to force building. If a SEAL platoon—or other organizational entity—specified a number, we figured simply multiply that by the numbers of "things." Pretty honest way to depict what was needed for a combat deployment except for "my wife, she, my car, it, my operation during mount out . . ."To ensure a required number of healthy SEALs were available, the manning documents needed to reflect a 10 percent overage to cover the potential slack/unavailable personnel. We learned Rangers man to 110 percent. This reality I needed to express to General Lindsay during one of his visits to the West Coast. With sweaty palms, I laid out our storage, which he assumed with tranquility. He'd seen it before. We were just shy of telling the king he was naked! Or, that my fear. Looking back at 1983 and that Saturday POM conference with Admiral Walters, I was conscious of having done it by haves . . . honest gut short of the mark. We finally got it right. There were no further surprises in the POM drills. Later, funding got tight. We needed to cut some things. SEAL Delivery Vehicle (SDV) Mark IX, a two-man submersible capable of launching torpedoes, was dropped from the armory. The MK VIII continued as the primary

SVD capable of transporting four men to an insertion point. I don't think a sigh of regret was uttered.

Then, one day, the Command got word that Secretary of Defense (SECDEF), the Honorable Dick Cheney, was coming to San Diego and wanted a SEAL presentation. He wasn't interested in view graphs, which he gets plenty of in his office. He wanted to see some gear and talk with troops. I asked Captain Ray Smith, COMNAVSPECWARGU ONE, to lay out a static display on the Amphibious Base Turner Field. We laid out diving gear, parachutes, small arms, communication equipment, night vision goggles, and sundry inflatable boats—Rigid Hull Inflatable Boats (RHIB) and ZODIAC Inflatable Boats, Small (IBS). He spent over thirty minutes chatting with the Platoon SEALs—with no interference from command or senior staffers—the unabridged version. He was knowledgeable and personable. I think the guys enjoyed his visit. On the way back after the static display, I rode in the sedan with him; he asked me if the USSOCOM set up was working. I was comfortable with the question said Navy was still getting Amphib SEALs, and the Joint Commands were happy with the product we deployed. Vis-à-vis requirements and budget, I gave him an example. Some SEALs might want super- duper SDV. They submit the formal Operational Requirement through SOCOM—although it will be 100 percent funded by Navy—to Navy. It makes total sense that the owner of the submarines this thing will deploy on should give it a scrub and thumbs up. The Air Force Special Ops Command wants in invisible "Wonder Woman" airplane. The Service "Senior Pilot" should get a chop on it; he's paying for it, and Air Force people will fly it and repair it. I told Cheney SOCOM was working, 2016 will mark thirty years SOCOM has been operational. I believe the command and its subordinate commands have acquitted themselves brilliantly.

In 1984, Captain Cathal "Irish" Flynn was selected to flag rank. I've already commented on how I thought he should gave stood up NAVSPECEARCOM. I think Navy missed a good leader and a marvelous public relations coup. After I relieved Chuck Le Moyne, he was selected to Upper Half, two stars. I had occasion to escort the CNO Admiral Frank Kelso, to a meeting of the Defense Special Operations Advisory Board. A couple of retired CIA Directors were members, like William Colby among others. Other SOF luminaries were included. Walking to the conference room, Admiral Kelso mentioned off-hand that he didn't think the SEAL community needed more than one two-star. Harrumph. That was it for my future in the Navy. That delightful news was late 1991. Soon after, I got a call from BUPERS, whom I knew, asking when could he expect my retirement letter. The unwritten law was if not promoted in two boards you would be asked to retire. I went out September 1, 1992. My relief, Ray Smith, was later promoted. And twenty years later, we had thirteen admirals—two four stars, several three, a bushel of twos, and a "fire team" gaggle of ones. Two of our full admirals commanded USSOCOM. One three-star was the SECDEF personal aide. One of our present flags is President Naval War College in Newport, R.I. (my former aide, Gardner Howe). It's safe to opine that Naval Special Warfare has come of age—the title of a Naval Institute *Proceedings* article by Irish Flynn in the late sixties. My end of tour award of the Navy Distinguished Service Medal speaks to my continued potential. But personnel management has its own dynamic. No sour grapes here.

One of the more delightful duties at the Command was getting ready for the annual SOCOM exposition in Tampa. It was a great opportunity to see what industry was cooking up. They, of course, wanted to learn all out needs, which I always suspected revealed our weaknesses. As I mentioned previously, we dive German 02

SCUBA, ride in French ZODIACs, and shoot German small arms. Our Development Group acquires top of the line equipment. And stemming from 9/11 funding has been available—entirely unlike my 1966 experience trying to buy a couple of Evenrude outboard engines. As for small arms, the Teams enjoy the best today; unlike my weapon in OPERATION JACKSTAY, a World War II grease gun. I retired at my final change of command, just before Labor Day. The thirty-one-year cruise was over, "Double up all lines."

What'd I learn? As a final three-year tour it was further impressed on me to stay timely with issues. This means not to shy away from controversy; it comes with the territory. One example today, "women in combat." This issue devolves to allowing women into front line ups and with this opening all combat training schools to women. We may be overtaken by events on this issue; personally I can't see women in a SEALs Team rubber boat or subjected to the rough life in the training command. But when the issue is decided, we'll salute with a hearty, "Aye, aye." But this is the response expected with all orders; it means, "I hear the order and will carry it out." In the Navy, it's taught constantly from the first day in uniform. (Another note on responses: if one doesn't know the answer to a question, the response is not "I don't know"; it's "I'll find out, Sir.") The learning point from flag service is get the facts right and deftly husband the staffing effort through the proper channels. Here, as with so many other things, diplomacy counts. I guess this translates into each staff section has to evaluate the fiscal and administrative impacts of an initiative/ issue and needs to win—or at last not lose anything. Thirty-plus years of service culminating in flag selection has to generate some appreciation for politics. I observed this collaborating with SOCOOM subordinate commanders.

Summer 1989, parachute requals at Marana, Arizona.

Jump over—debrief and repack.

Christmas 1990 with family at Club Med Colorado.

1992 Training from a USAF C5 over Scotland.

1990 Army - Navy Game, Philadelphia

Change of command comments with
General Carl Stiner, USA, my last boss.

CHAPTER 16

THE FINAL PHASE—RETIREMENT AND GETTING ON WITH LIFE

Getting on with life has proven almost as challenging as active duty. The first realization to hit home was how long it took/ takes to get something done, not that I was a proficient multi-tasker; but it seems as if routine events—paying bills, watering the lawn, grocery shopping, reading emails—all feel like center stage events. Then, as I age, I sometime wonder what I walked into a room for. Time allocation and measurement have taken on a new dimension. Sounds familiar?

1992 was seemingly unimpressive as a year. Islamic plane hijackings were the international events *du jour*. The "Blind Sheik" was a year away from his World Trade Center attack. The election that year pitted sitting President George Bush against the Clinton machine—futile battle as it turned out; but here we are again (2015) with the "rerun." The first days of retirement were like a long holiday weekend. Cast about for some kind of defense work, sending out a few resumes to local contractors with little response. I was offered spots on two boards—ZODIAC of North America, purveyors of SEAL rubber boats, out of Stevensville, Maryland; and WEXCAM-Sonoma, manufacturers of high resolution camera mounts for Predator UAVs. Both positions were enjoyable and edifying.

Next work relating, was an offer from an outfit called "WarRoom Research," basically a "Dot-Com" enterprise out of Baltimore that strove to create dedicated war room technology that included a business-oriented intelligence internet portal. Among other pursuits I was on was a high-tech advisory board in Silicon Valley producing broad ban frequency jamming equipment. The terror attack scenario was ramping up. We questioned what happens when a remotely piloted model plane or missile is launched at the White House. (Might as well start at the top.) We filmed a model airplane in a lab setting go berserk when jammed, potentially deflecting the plane from the White House. We were invited to demonstrate the capability at the Secret Service Campus in Maryland. The field guys liked it; the Service R&D rep did not and warned us off lest our clearances be confiscated—a boldface threat like I had never experienced before. And look at all.

Around 1995, I was still burdened by an attachment to Naval Special Warfare. One of the things that community needed was a dedicated ship beyond the occasional Amphib taxi. A friend had designed a mono-hull, high-speed combatant craft, designated "H-3". His family had spent a lot of money getting it designed. We saw an opening and went to a breakfast with Congressman Duncan Hunter and convinced him the requirement for an inshore craft for inserting SEALs and other Special Operations Forces (SOF). He liked the idea and supported some seed monies to develop a prototype. He got an acquaintance at Naval Research to sponsor the effort. Along the way, the Marine Corps came in the backdoor with a need for a helicopter platform just outside the surf zone that could rearm and refuel choppers in close support of engaged troops on the beach. The flat deck eliminated H-3. English ferry designer, Gee, was contracted to design something—the result, a 200 foot catamaran capable of fifty-plus knots, ultimately titled "Sea Fighter." Built, launched, and floated in 2005, we thought the ship would create a revolution in surface ship design. At the same moment in time, the "Littoral Combat Ship" was competing with big industry for service acceptance. All this "inshore" business got first introduced back in 1990 in a Navy White Paper titled, *Forward . . . from the Sea*. For a decade it was all lip service; Sea Fighter was launched whilst the white ink was still wet on NAVSEA blueprints. We were pushing a craft that could support SEAL Team and Special Boat operations. An extracting stern ramp would permit launch and recovery of combatant craft (Rigid Inflatable Rubber Boats—ZODIACs, for example). Two helicopter spots on the flat deck would pick up men and equipment and refuel those off-shore Marine Corps choppers. We always joked that our (Gee's) design was outflanked by "K Street" interests—the bivouac address of the "Big Boys," the industry go-to shipbuilding giants. The Navy ended up with a Littoral Combat Ship (LCS), a dual design competitive class that has never measured up to its mission statement. And the SEALs are still hitchhiking on the Amphibious Force or an occasional destroyer. We get better service from the Submarine Force.

Rotary wing support is another sore spot. During Vietnam SEALs operated from Helicopter Attack, Light (HAL) Squadrons. They stuck around flying Hueys for many years in the Reserves. We took them overseas. Then, Secretary John Lehman approved some Navy version HH-60 choppers. I rode in one of the first in the fall of 1985. I had just assumed command of NSWG-1. It proved to be a short-lived mirage. Navy took them to sea on carries and Naval Special Warfare was back taking a ticket. The late nineties saw two SpecsOps RW Squadrons, which of this writing are going away. Stand in line to exercise helo insertion/extraction techniques. And it's the ari crews that need to rehears close-in flying. Marine chopper pilots do this all the time; Navy less so. I've already discussed the issue; it needs to be solved. In point of fact, the Naval Special Warfare Groups are nowhere near the USSOCOM aviation bases. I can't remember the last time Army or Air Force rotary wing assets deployed to a Naval Base for a joint training event. It's a glaring gap in capability. In the meantime, the Joint High Speed Vessel program has potential for the Afloat Forward Staging Base (ASFB) called out in the FY-2006 Quarterly Defense Review (QDR). To remind, the QDR stated, "Special Operations Forces will exploit Afloat Forwarding Staging Base (AFSB) to provide more flexible and sustainable locations from which to operate globally." The Hill told USSOCOM to do it; but it turns out it's a Navy (Service) commitment, financially and engineering-wise. A distinct Special Operations mission protocol needs to be scripted to define how these craft will operate with SOF.

Around 1997 I got an invitation to join the Board of Directors of the Special Operations Warrior Foundation, a "not for profit" foundation dedicated to providing full college scholarships to the children of SOF personnel killed in training and combat. The SOWF was started by Air Force people following the disaster at DESERT ONE during the 1980 putative hostage rescue operation. It was chaired by Retired Air Force Lieutenant General LeRoy Manor and boasted such members as former Army Chief of Staff "Shy" Meyer—a principal supporter of SOCOM and Hal Steinbrenner, today head of the New York Yankees. Following an internal personnel and organization dust-up, former Air Force Commando John Carney took over as president and the foundation flourished. I served twelve years before moving on. Today, Retired Vice Admiral Joe Maguire heads the show.

During the early 2000s, I had the honor of doing chapters on Naval Special Warfare for two photobooks, "The United States Navy" and "United States Special Operations Forces." In the fall of 2006, photo journalist Greg Mathieson invited me to write for a photo-anthology he was preparing with U.S. Naval Institute sponsorship. It would have to pass muster with the Naval Special Warfare Command in order to gain support from subordinate SEAL commands. Then Commander Rear Admiral Joe Maguire heard our pitch, in which we assured him every word and photo would be screened by his people for security and appropriateness—and approved the effort. I suspect the USNI participation was essential. Greg had been trying for years to get a "go ahead" on the effort. Maguire informed the Groups. Of course, I was well-known as a "runner with frogs" over the years. Possibly the Navy and SPECOPs books helped out as well. In fact, I needed command approval to get photos and interview permission for those books. Our latest effort would end up taking six years! I invited the NSW SEAL community "historian" commander, Tom Hawkins, to jump in with history and other chapters he might be interested in. We knocked out the original tome in about a year. Production proved harder than "Runnin' with Frogs!" From "dry ink" in 2007, it took five more years to get it published. With leviathan efforts from Greg and a home mortgage, we got out in December 2012 on the fiftieth anniversary of SEAL Teams.

This book goes beyond SEAL and Special Boat Teams; it delves into the supporting specialties that keep the Teams and operators on the line. Communications, logistics and supply, intelligence, fiscal, personnel, research and development, administration and of course, the training command. It weighs in over eight pounds. Greg finagled a letter from former President George Bush, a foreword by former SECNAV John Lehman, and a "Futures" chapter by Former SECNAV Donald Winter. It's a slick book that emphasizes the unsung warriors in the paper trenches. The reader will be impressed with the diversity reflected in the photography; many female sailors are assigned as technicians, which remains a sensitive subject at present on whether or not women should be assigned to frontline combat units.

French owned ZODIAC sold itself to an American interest obviating the need for domestic security oversight; WarRoom went bust with the rest of the internet bubble companies. "Will work for food!"

Then, in summer 2008, and invention to come to Bethesda, Maryland, and participate in the "Bethesda Hospital Emergency Preparedness Partnership," a lash-up of the U.S. Naval Medical Center, Suburban Hospital, The Institutes of Health, and the National Medical Library oriented on cooperation during emergencies affecting the National Command Region, Washington, D.C. and close-in area hospitals. By my arrival in late September, the partnership was functioning quite well. My take was the BHEPP was working fine with clear lines of organization and control. What could I add that was not already in place? One major area of consternation was the initial lack of an office beyond the security conference and my briefcase, not to mention the need to find a place to live. By my first Wednesday, I was ready to return home! The apartment issue cleared on a weekend, the office took two weeks. Clearly, my hiring was resisted. But I had a good Hell Week, and quitting wasn't in the lexicon. Truth be known, as I experienced it in the five months Bethesda wanted to fund me, hiring me was probably an afterthought.

None of the participants needed my beach recon expertise. I was able to generate interest in a couple of places, but, alas, nothing gets done in Washington without funding. BHEPP was slowly drying up. Hearts were in the right place, but in truth, BHEPP participation was an "elective" by the people assigned—extra time with no extra pay. But the experience was edifying, learning a bit about hospital administration. Unfortunately, the Congressional earmark that funded BHEPP was over mid-March . . . and I was gone.

Another interesting association I had was early 2000 involvement in the Vietnam Veterans' Memorial Fund and the effort of Vietnam founder, Jan Scruggs, to construct an Education Center next to the Wall—with a museum and artifact display left by survivors at the Wall. I was invited by Jan to join the board of advisors. As a Navy SEAL, he thought I might have an opinion—careful. One of the first things I did was recommend adding a medical representative—Doctor Steve Philipps, MD, a cardio-surgeon and Viet Vet with the 101st (Airborne), and then currently at the National Library of Medicine I Bethesda, Maryland—a perfect fit. The proposed Education Center is in its final phases of capital campaigning for funding and should break ground in fall 2016. (Watch me be wrong! It's been five years and a lot of schmoozing.) The "center" will celebrate Armed Forces from the Revolution to today, not Vietnam.

Since returning home in March 2009, I've been awkwardly learning to adapt to every retired day morphing into "Saturday." I read, write irate letters to the editor, dabble on a national security blog, and try to say in some sort of physical shape. But when you hit seventy-five it seems like you have to start changing out parts, that is, welcome the blade! Parachuting took its toll on my lower back, or at worst accelerated the arthritis. Ditto shoulders. I'm obliged now to keep fit in a more gentle fashion—no more bent over exercise but okay seated weight machines and reasonable swimming. And no more "max weight" events; higher repetitions with more measured weights, like 400 pull-downs with 50 pounds, reps into the fifties, etc. I workout but rarely need to break a sweat. As for skydiving, it's not the freefall or the sometimes-jerky opening but the danger of an off-site emergency landing or sometime-raggedy running landing coupled with a forced tumble. The flesh stops but the metal implants keep flying! (Not good.)

Finally, last month I became a first-time grandparent to a baby girl named Madeline; born to my SEAL son, Rhodes, and his wife, Maggie (Harward), on June 0, 2015 to the delight of both families. I plan on runnin' with frogs for awhile, yet I only to keep up! The experiences of the past fifty years (as my BUD/S class 36 celebrates "gold" this year), the road taken has been plentiful with people and adventure.

By way of a reiterative postscript, I will sum up with hopes for (1) dedicated SEAL helicopters, (2) dedicated surface ship for Naval Special Boats (SEAL and Boat Teams), and (3) a dry SEAL submarine delivery vehicle. I feel fortunate to have been a part of the eighties' defense revitalization effort, which continues today. I would also pray for a more placid era for the world, but that doesn't appear to be in the cards, regretfully. To recall the late sixties when Naval Special Warfare was seen as a truncated career path, the Special Operations community has come a long way. One-third of SEAL enlisted have college degrees (my son is one), and officers are competing for top slots, e.g., Admirals Olson and McRaven. (An Army SpecOps general was chairman.) The future is indeed bright. But there are warning signs on the way, the most important being the tendency to grow too large with bureaucracy. It was important during the eighties to recognize the need for technical support as systems became more sophisticated. Operating a submarine Dry Deck Shelter (DDS) requires "sub-safe" technical standards, which SEAL enlisted operators must be qualified to support. Boats are more specialized than the World War II LCPLs. "Rubber boats" are advanced beyond the "rafts." Frank Kaine dropped demo from in the Pacific campaign. In "the old days," Seals had to maintain Navy ratings to serve and advance—shipfitter, machinist, radioman, boilerman. Enlisted SEALs today have a unique SEAL Special Operations Rating. In the 2006 Quarterly Defense Review, Congress called for a 15 percent across-the-board expansion of Special Operations Forces. Naval Special Warfare was obliged to increase the Training Cadre for SEALs and Special Boat volunteers by expanding class accessions and number of classes per year. The NSW Training Command has to keep the increased instructor levels as 2006 to account for the increased force level. And these instructors have to come from the operational ranks—added to which normal attrition: medical (KIA, WIA, recovery), family emergencies, retirees. And then, too, there's the issue of females in combat, which impact has not yet influenced standards. At present, all SOF is most likely pushing the envelope of the potential volunteer population. But NSW is infrastructure limited. Even with an expanded campus south of Coronado, the training pool is stretched. So, beware the urge to believe SOF is appropriate to every rational security crises. Today, there are warnings about potential large scale military challenges—Ukraine, South China Sea, the Baltic States, North Korea, and Iran. SOF can play important supportive roles, but getting too heavy administratively might detract from the "special" of the title.

Those left will still be "Runnin' with Frogs"—as I hope to be in the years ahead.

POST SERVICE PHOTOS

As a member of the Vietnam Wall Education Center initiative,
conference to select a contractor—Jan Scruggs in the foreground.

Evening reception and dinner before the Education Congressional
Hearing. In attendance is actor Robert Duval, ardent Center supporter—
Scruggs in the background.

Veterans' Day 1996 at the Vietnam Wall. To my left are Jan Scruggs, founder of the Wall; and Jim Kimsey, West Point 1962, co-founder of America Online.

October . . . a Dracula jump.

Accompanying my son's first jump—a tandem from 13,000 feet. He later
did the jump course in three days. We later did jumps together.

1995, a trip to Vietnam. Sa Dec, south of Ho Chi Minh City (Saigon), visit
with a former VC Province Chief (lost his right eye) and local functionary;
lady, Luan Shell, was an officer With the Swiss "Feed the Children."

Bustling, industrious Hanoi.

February 2010. As part of the Stefan Banic Parachute Foundation, presenting former President George Bush with a gold medal for his espousing the spot of skydiving.

Son's graduation from SEAL Qualification Training (June 10, 2011).

Nurses in the Sa Dec clinic. Chided by our medical escort who spoke
Vietnamese, French, and English, for always being in the lab, never with
patients. Dogs roamed the corridors. But they vaccinate over 95 percent
of children for hepatitis.

Kiddos along the Saigon-Sa Dec route—same the world over.

Along the road to Vung Tau. Young entrepreneur hawking cokes. By 1995, twenty years after I left Phnom Penh, the Vietnamese population had doubled.

A youngster by the lake at Hanoi. I walked everywhere, even found the
Irish Bar "The Emerald."

Saigon (HCMC) Rex Rooftop. Still vibrant.

Hanoi: McCain statue.
The Senator, whose office arranged our visas, has been to it.

Vung Tau beach with European vacationers.

Active service over—time for fun. Skydiving over southern
California at Skydive San Diego.

We put Sea Fighter in the water for under a hundred million.

Sea Fighter—an experimental hull for a
Naval Special Warfare support craft in the littoral.

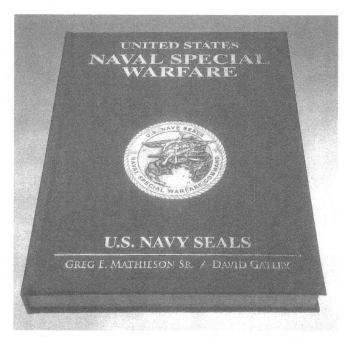

Commenced work on all-encompassing Naval Special Warfare photo-
anthology. After fits and starts and with Command approval and support,
the eight-pound tome was published in December 2012, on the fiftieth
anniversary of U.S. Navy SEAL Teams.

"The only easy day was yesterday."

CPSIA information can be obtained
at www.ICGtesting.com
Printed in the USA
LVHW092143020321
680439LV00004B/28